Dictatorship

This book analyses the institution and concept of dictatorship from a legal, historical and theoretical perspective, examining the different types of dictatorship, their relationship to the law, as well as the analytical value of the concept in the contemporary world.

In particular, it seeks to codify the main theories and conceptions of 'dictatorship', with the goal of unearthing their contradictions. The main premise is that the concept of dictatorship and the different types of the dictatorial form have to be assessed and can only be understood in their historical context. On this basis, the elaborations on dictatorship of such diverse thinkers as Carl Schmitt, Donoso Cortés, Karl Marx, Ernst Fraenkel, Franz Neumann, Nicos Poulantzas and V.I. Lenin are discussed in their historical context: 'classical and Caesaristic dictatorship' in ancient Rome, 'dictatorship' in revolutionary France of 1789 and counterrevolutionary France of 1848, 'fascist dictatorship' in Nazi Germany, and 'dictatorship of the proletariat' in Russia of 1917. The book contributes to the theory of dictatorship as it outlines the contradictions of the different typologies of the dictatorial form and seeks to explain them on the basis of the concept of 'class dictatorship'. The book's original claim is that the dictatorial form, as a modality of class rule that relies predominantly on violence and repression, has been essential to the reproduction of bourgeois rule and, consequently, of capitalist social relations. This function has given rise to different types and conceptualisations of dictatorship depending on the level of capitalist development.

This book is addressed to anyone with an interest in law, political theory, political history and sociology. It can serve as a core text for courses that seek to introduce students to the institution or theory of dictatorship. It may also serve as a reference text for post-graduate programs in law and politics because of its interdisciplinary and critical approach.

Dimitrios Kivotidis is a Lecturer in Public Law at University of East London.

**Part of the
NEW TRAJECTORIES IN LAW
series**
series editors
Adam Gearey, Birkbeck College, University of London
Colin Perrin, Commissioning Editor, Routledge

for information about the series and details of previous and forthcoming titles, see www.routledge.com/New-Trajectories-in-Law/book-series/NTL

A GlassHouse Book

Dictatorship
New Trajectories in Law

Dimitrios Kivotidis

a GlassHouse Book

First published 2021
by Routledge
2 Park Square, Milton Park, Abingdon, Oxon OX14 4RN

and by Routledge
52 Vanderbilt Avenue, New York, NY 10017
A GlassHouse book

Routledge is an imprint of the Taylor & Francis Group, an informa business

© 2021 Dimitrios Kivotidis

The right of Dimitrios Kivotidis to be identified as author of this work has been asserted by him in accordance with sections 77 and 78 of the Copyright, Designs and Patents Act 1988.

All rights reserved. No part of this book may be reprinted or reproduced or utilised in any form or by any electronic, mechanical, or other means, now known or hereafter invented, including photocopying and recording, or in any information storage or retrieval system, without permission in writing from the publishers.

Trademark notice: Product or corporate names may be trademarks or registered trademarks, and are used only for identification and explanation without intent to infringe.

British Library Cataloguing-in-Publication Data
A catalogue record for this book is available from the British Library

Library of Congress Cataloging-in-Publication Data
Names: Kivotidis, Dimitrios, author.
Title: Dictatorship: new trajectories in law / Dimitrios Kivotidis.
Description: Abingdon, Oxon; New York, NY: Routledge, 2021. |
Series: New trajectories in law | Includes bibliographical references and index.
Identifiers: LCCN 2020040752 (print) | LCCN 2020040753 (ebook) |
ISBN 9780367460365 (hardback) | ISBN 9781003145974 (ebook)
Subjects: LCSH: Dictatorship. | Middle class–Political activity.
Classification: LCC JC495 .K58 2021 (print) | LCC JC495 (ebook) |
DDC 321.9–dc23
LC record available at https://lccn.loc.gov/2020040752
LC ebook record available at https://lccn.loc.gov/2020040753

ISBN: 978-0-367-46036-5 (hbk)
ISBN: 978-0-367-70378-3 (pbk)
ISBN: 978-1-003-14597-4 (ebk)

Typeset in Times New Roman
by Newgen Publishing UK

Frontispiece credit: Image by Orfeas-Vasilis Kivotidis

To Stavros

Contents

Acknowledgements   viii

Introduction   1

1   **Historical and theoretical foundations**   8
Roman dictatorship 10
Commissarial and sovereign dictatorship 14
Exception, emergency, necessity 22

2   **Dictatorship and consolidation of bourgeois power**   29
Modern dictatorship 29
Bonapartism, Caesarism and dictatorship 35
Dictatorship and crisis of hegemony 39

3   **Dictatorship and reproduction of bourgeois power**   47
Nazi dictatorship 48
Nazism as totalitarianism 53
Nazism as Caesarism 58
Nazism as Fascism 64

4   **Dictatorship and the supersession of the bourgeois state**   73
Dictatorship as class rule 74
Reopening the debate on Marxist 'dictatorship' 79
Dictatorship of the proletariat 89

5   **Contribution to the theory of dictatorship**   101

6   **Theses on the concept of dictatorship**   120

Index   124

Acknowledgements

No research is carried out in a vacuum. I have been very lucky to be a member of various research groups and communities over the last decade, the members of which to a varying extent have influenced the thoughts and ideas expressed in this book. Special thanks are always due to Georgios Kolias, my brother in arms, and Alexandros Giannakouras, my very own gadfly.

For the last couple of years I have been blessed to be in the good company of the editorial collective of Legal Form, so many thanks are due to Paul O'Connell, Umut Özsu, Jasmine Chorley Foster, Rob Hunter and Eva Nanopoulos. Paul deserves an independent mention as he has had my back every step of the way. The collective work of this group has encouraged me to continue pursuing a Marxist analysis of the legal form. Various themes explored in this book have been developed in several instalments of the Critical Legal Conference, but always in the panels organised by Cosmin Cercel, in the good company of Gian Giacomo Fusco, Simon Lavis, Ceylan Begüm Yıldız and Rafał Manko. Cosmin also deserves an independent mention as he encouraged me to write on this specific topic.

I would also like to thank my friends and colleagues at Birkbeck Law School, especially Paddy McDaid, Ozan Kamiloglou, Marcus Vinicius de Matos, Kojo Koram, Tara Mulqueen, Leticia Paes, Enrique Rios, Natalia Delgado, Kanika Sharma, Mayur Suresh and everyone else I may have forgotten, who set the highest standards of friendship and comradeship. Many thanks are also due to Costas Douzinas, who gave me the opportunity to begin this journey in academia. I also want to thank Stewart Motha for all his help, as well as Thanos Zartaloudis for his delicate presence at various difficult moments.

Last but not least, I would like to thank Adam Geary and Colin Perrin for their constant support and patience with this project.

Introduction

The overthrow of the Eastern Bloc and the Soviet regimes at the end of the twentieth century was celebrated by theorists of the 'end of history'[1] as a victory of the Western model of the liberal-democratic state against dictatorship and totalitarianism. This interpretation is still dominant today as the portrayal of Mao and Stalin as dictators—even more so than Hitler—is widely accepted by the Western cultural environment, mainstream media and popular opinion. However, even after the 'end of history', military interventions around the world have been carried out against dictatorial regimes (such as Muammar Gaddafi's in Libya, Saddam Hussein's in Iraq, or Bashar al-Assad's in Syria) in the name of democracy and human rights, whereas other potential enemies of the global order and the United States' hegemonic role in it (such as Vladimir Putin in Russia, and Kim Jong-un in North Korea) have also been portrayed as dictators.

Furthermore, the liberal-democratic West has undergone an equally frightening process over the last decade, following the global financial crisis of 2008, namely, the rise of far-right-wing parties that mask authoritarian, racist and fascist ideologies under populist propaganda. These parties are the political offspring of those that have been historically associated with dictatorial regimes in Europe, and they have reignited the debate on the relationship between authoritarianism and democracy. How tolerant can liberal democracy be towards authoritarian parties? How can democracy defend itself against parties that may preach its overthrow? These questions have troubled political theorists and the public over the few centuries of the existence of bourgeois states and are directly related to the concept of dictatorship. After

---

1 See Francis Fukuyama, *The End of History and the Last Man* (London: Penguin, 2012).

all, dictatorship was originally an institution of the Roman Republic, designed to protect it against existential threats.

What is more, these movements and parties have arisen in the context of a tendency of the Western liberal-democratic state itself to assume a more authoritarian form, in a process that began a few decades ago, described by Nicos Poulantzas as authoritarian statism.[2] This process involves the insulation of decision-making processes from the popular strata and the conferral of crucial competences to unaccountable institutions that decide on issues with far-reaching consequences for social and economic relations. These processes have been criticised as assaults on the democratic nature of the nation state. However, is 'dictatorship' an accurate term to use for the critique of such processes? What is the relationship between dictatorship and authoritarianism? What is the meaning of the old, almost-forgotten term of the dictatorship of the bourgeoisie, and can it be of any help in analysing the current predicament?

Recently, the prorogation of the British Parliament by the Queen on the advice of the Prime Minister was attacked by various politicians, the media and a great number of the British people as a dictatorship and a suspension of democracy. The phrase #*thisisacoup* flooded social media—and not for the first time in the recent past. In the interest of scientific accuracy, one has to ask: Is the British Parliament democratic? Does it operate based on the democratic principle? Can it be considered a stronghold of democratic rule? Of course the democratic principle operates in the British political system and is reflected in the British constitutional arrangement, for instance, in the development of constitutional conventions such as the one according to which the Queen appoints as Prime Minister the leader of the party that wins the majority in the House of Commons following a general election. Nevertheless, the British Parliament is a bicameral parliament that essentially consists of three bodies—the Crown, the Lords and the Commons. Sovereignty of parliament as the cornerstone of the British constitution means that Parliament is vested with absolute power and unconditional authority. This fact led Donoso Cortés, in his famous 'Speech on Dictatorship' in 1848, to declare the British Parliament as the exemplary dictatorial institution.[3] What, then, is more dictatorial, the power of the British Parliament or the instrumental use of established practices—such as

---

[2] Nicos Poulantzas, *State, Power, Socialism* (London: Verso, 2014).
[3] Donoso Cortés, 'Speech on Dictatorship', in *Selected Works of Juan Donoso Cortés* (London: Greenwood Press, 2000), 45–60.

prorogation—by an executive that presents itself as the exponent of the people's will?

As the Brexit drama plays out, different individuals and different social groups, pretending to express either the will of the people or the will of Parliament, have made claims of democratic legitimacy accusing the other party of dictatorial practices. Concepts such as democracy and dictatorship are used as trenches for intra-class warfare, while the popular strata will suffer the worst consequences of any solution to this drama. On this basis, this book aspires to be a modest contribution to the scientific analysis of juridico-political terms, which I believe is an essential prerequisite for meaningful juridico-political debate. Otherwise fundamental concepts must remain empty signifiers that are instrumentalised by political opportunism. Of course, I do not claim political or ideological purity. On the contrary, I believe that science is political, to the extent that scientific results tending to accurate analyses of objective reality (i.e. of natural and social processes) support or thwart the struggle of particular classes.

This book is written with a deep conviction that a clear understanding of the concept of dictatorship is crucial to make sense of several processes in the legal and political sphere taking place currently throughout the world. For this reason, it undertakes the interesting and challenging task of documenting the evolution of this concept in conjunction with several related concepts (such as state of exception, Caesarism, Bonapartism and totalitarianism) in different historical situations. The work of different theorists from different eras and different standpoints—such as Donoso Cortés, Carl Schmitt, Giorgio Agamben, Claude Nicolet, Melvin Richter, Antonio Gramsci, Nicos Poulantzas and Hal Draper—is discussed. All these thinkers have come up with different concepts and methods to conceptualise 'dictatorship' and examine its historical, theoretical, social and economic origins.

This work follows the dialectical method of analysis, focusing on the contradictions that are reproduced by a specific form. The main purpose is to highlight the contradictions of the formal theories of dictatorship. Dialectical materialism refers to a mode of conceiving reality in its many-sided and contradictory movements. Therefore, a dialectical analysis of the dictatorial form takes into account the intricate relations between legal, political and socio-economic processes, as opposed to the isolated and fragmented way of examining legal phenomena by positivist theory. Additionally, social, political and juridical processes are seen as historical processes. Capitalism, law and the state are not eternal structures. They are, rather, historical phenomena. So, the examination of dictatorship has to take into account the historical movement: how the dictatorial form has developed historically with regards to socio-economic development. Last but not least, the historical movement of juridico-political and socio-economic processes examined develops on the basis of antagonistic contradictions and struggle of the opposites. The dialectical analysis will combine legal and theoretical material, which will be assessed in their historical context, to explain the specific function of dictatorship in the consolidation, reproduction and supersession of the contradictory relations of capitalism.

The change in the meaning of dictatorship from ancient Rome to early modernity is well documented. The concept of dictatorship had vanished from political analyses and legal treatises for several centuries after the last phase of the Roman Republic and the dictatorships of Sulla and Caesar. There is a very good reason for this disappearance. It had to do with the modes of exercise of public power in feudal society that rested predominantly on divine authority, rather than popular legitimation. The concept of dictatorship re-emerges in early modernity and gains increasing significance after the French Revolution and the establishment and consolidation of bourgeois rule. From an institution essential to the Republic in ancient Rome to a type of regime that is entirely antithetical to democracy in the twentieth century, there are certain similarities that are captured by the concept of dictatorship. This study will locate these similarities and discuss the reasons for this change in meaning. In doing so, it will situate the discussion in the existing literature on this concept and the juridico-political analyses of the historical situations described by it. In codifying these theories, this book will advance the author's own approach on the concept, emphasising a re-evaluation of the Marxist concept of class dictatorship and its relevance in analysing contemporary juridico-political phenomena.

On this basis, the book deals with interrelated questions, such as:

- How has the concept of dictatorship been used historically?
- Which types of dictatorship have been conceptualised and what other terms have been used to describe this phenomenon?
- What is dictatorship's relationship to the law according to different theorists?
- Does the concept of dictatorship have analytical value in the contemporary world?

This book will assess the historical meaning of the term in relation to the levels of capitalist development. The view that there is an extra-historical meaning of the term is rejected. Instead this study examines how this concept has been used to describe different forms of exercise of public power. At the same time, it avoids an absolute relativisation of the concept and seeks to outline the lines of continuity of its use, linking it to the different forms of exercise of public power as determined by the different phases in the consolidation of bourgeois rule.

Taking into account the different types of dictatorship that have been proposed by different theorists (Caesaristic, totalitarian, military, commissarial, sovereign, etc.), there are two main ways this concept has been used: *one* is to describe the institution that is found in almost every constitutional structure and is known as state of siege, state of exception or state of emergency; the other is to describe a type of authoritarian regime that is mostly based on force rather than consent, on executive decision-making rather than parliamentary processes and on centralisation of power rather than on liberal separation of powers. The common element between these two forms is an element of temporariness and transitionality. Both dictatorial forms (states of emergency and dictatorial regimes) result from crises (political, socio-economic or, most commonly, a combination of both) that necessitate a change in the form of exercise of public power.

However, a central problem arises as there is a tendency, first, of one type of dictatorship to give way to the other. To take the Nazi dictatorship as an example, the state of emergency declared in February 1933 gave way to the establishment of a dictatorial regime tout court with the Enabling Act of March 1933. Second, the element of temporariness is consequently relativised, as the establishment of dictatorial regimes themselves, despite their initially commissarial character, leads to—in fact, it satisfies a demand for—new normality and permanence. On this basis, I approach dictatorship as a *modus operandi* of state power and as a form of exercise of class rule, to address the central issue of continuity between normal and dictatorial state forms. This approach will enable the move beyond the contradictions of temporality between the two main types of dictatorship.

Thus, dictatorship signifies a mode of class rule whereby the bourgeois state adjusts its form (temporarily or permanently, depending on whether the dictatorial institutions have the right to enact legislation, as well as on their source of legitimacy) to reproduce itself (as well as the regime of power, property and production relations). The equivocation between the two main types (state of emergency and dictatorial regime) is due to the far-reaching nature of changes that a crisis may necessitate for social relations to be reproduced. Thus, analysing the contradictions and equivocation between the different types of dictatorship presupposes an examination of the conditions that necessitate dictatorial solutions. This is where Marxist analyses of dictatorship are relevant.

Dictatorship becomes essential in situations of crisis when there is a need for the state to step forward and take an active role in the consolidation or reproduction of the capitalist relations of production, through increase of its relative autonomy.[4] The particular characteristics of the dictatorial form are determined by the level of development of capitalism. But in all different phases of capitalism, a dictatorial form has resulted from a process of devaluation of existing representative political institutions and the need for replacement by other institutions (existing or newly created). For instance, both in the 1850s and the 1930s, the vulgar depreciation of Parliament led to the increasing use of plebiscites. To this end, a discussion of Gramsci's analysis of Caesarism and hegemony and Poulantzas's analysis of fascism will provide the book with a theoretical framework to examine the relationship between the different types of dictatorship and the law.

Understanding dictatorship as a mode of exercise of class rule is crucial for grasping the unity between norm and exception in jurisprudential terms. For instance, the Nazi state form cannot be grasped merely as the dictatorial antithesis to the normal form of the Weimar Republic. On the contrary, if the Weimar form was the old normality, the Nazi form was a new normality insofar as it guaranteed the uninterrupted continuity of bourgeois rule and capitalist production. In conditions that threaten the reproduction of capitalist social relations, a dictatorship restores the normality by crushing the class-conscious workers' movement. As Donoso Cortés put it as early as 1848, 'when the letter of the law is enough to save a society, then the letter of the law is best, but when it is not enough, then dictatorship is best'.[5]

---

[4] Relative autonomy is a central concept for the Marxist analysis of state and law. It is necessary for the state to act as a factor of cohesion and consolidation of class power (intra-class aspect), as well as for the effective exercise of class rule (class aspect). As E.P. Thompson puts it with regards to the latter, the essential precondition for the effectiveness of law, in its function as ideology, is that it shall display an independence from gross manipulation and shall seem to be just; if the law is evidently partial and unjust, then it will mask nothing, legitimise nothing, contribute nothing to any class's hegemony; see E.P. Thompson, *Whigs and Hunters* (London: Breviary Stuff Publications, 2013), 263. Along the same lines with regards to the former, according to Poulantzas, capitalist law appears as 'the necessary form of a State that has to maintain relative autonomy of the fractions of a power-bloc in order to organize their unity under the hegemony of a given class or fraction'; see Poulantzas, *State, Power, Socialism*, 91.

[5] Cortés, *Speech on Dictatorship*, 45–60.

The concept of *salus populi* underlies both liberal-democratic states and dictatorial regimes, both normal and exceptional state forms. *Salus populi suprema lex* is a maxim that translates into 'the safety or welfare of the people should be the highest law'. This Roman maxim is the origin of all relevant public law concepts used to justify a restriction, limitation or suspension of rights on the basis of general interest or national security. *Salus populi* is society's salvation from its enemies. *Salus populi*, or the common good, is the main formal justification of the dictatorial form. But its operation is central in conditions of normality, too, as the concept of *salus populi* appears and shapes the courts' jurisprudence, especially during crises. This point is of great importance to grasp the contemporary significance of the concept of dictatorship. This is what the last chapter of the book will explore: dictatorship as part of a system of gradations of authoritarianism, the specific form of which is determined by the level of capitalist development and the development of class struggle in specific countries. Insofar as the reproduction of capitalist social relations can be accomplished predominantly on the basis of ideological, consensual means, resort to a dictatorial regime *tout court* is not necessary.

With regards to the scope of the historical cases analysed in the book, they focus almost exclusively on European history. This is done strictly for reasons of brevity—as the book is meant to be a contribution to the theory of dictatorship rather than an exhaustive analysis of its historical instantiations—and clarity of the argument. The book is structured with a view to examining the reasons for the re-emergence of the concept in early modernity and its use and function in different periods of crisis of capitalist society. Therefore, the main historical conjunctions dealt with are: ancient Rome and the origins of the concept; revolutionary France in 1789 and counter-revolutionary France in 1848, and the use of the concept during the establishment and consolidation of bourgeois rule; Nazi Germany and the reproduction of bourgeois rule in a situation of acute crisis; and the use of the concept in Marxist theories for the supersession of capitalism, with a focus on the Paris Commune of 1871 and the October Revolution of 1917. Nevertheless, one of the aims of the book is to show that the methodological approach and general theoretical conclusions can be used to analyse dictatorial regimes and institutions throughout the world.

1 Historical and theoretical foundations

The popular understanding of dictatorship refers to a type of regime that is oppressive because of its reliance on the use of violence. Since all modern states in the last instance rely on violence (the state itself being the apparatus that monopolistically exercises violence in a legitimate manner), violence in itself cannot be the distinguishing characteristic of a dictatorship. Violence is accompanied by arbitrariness and an absence of respect for individual rights and due process (i.e. the absence of constitutional limits to the exercise of public power). Furthermore, perhaps the most commonly understood characteristic of the idea of dictatorship is its anti-democratic nature. Dictatorship is identified with a lack of representative institutions and the concentration of power in the hands of a ruler, the dictator. Personal rule and concentration of power have long been considered as the essential characteristics of the common-sense meaning of dictatorship.[1] The fact that usually a dictatorship is signified just by the name of the dictator (Hitler, Mussolini, Franco, etc.) attests to this.

If modern-day, common-sense understanding of the idea of dictatorship opposes democratic government to it, this was not always so. In the days of consolidation of bourgeois power, during the period of the forging of the modern bourgeois states, dictatorship was seen as an aspect of the democratic movement.[2] In fact, dictatorship was used in a pejorative way to describe representative institutions themselves. During the French Revolution, the Girondins used the term to denounce the 'dictatorship of the National Convention' (i.e. the exemplary institution of revolutionary democracy), or the 'dictatorship of

---

1 Carl Schmitt, *Dictatorship* (London: Polity Press, 2013), xxxviii.
2 Hal Draper, *The Dictatorship of the Proletariat from Marx to Lenin* (New York: Monthly Review Press, 1987), 14.

the Commune of Paris', which was the most democratic expression yet seen of a mass movement from below.[3] In 1848 Donoso Cortés, in his famous speech on dictatorship, used the term to describe the British Parliament whose omnipotence is precisely what constitutes 'dictatorial power'.[4] In the 1850s dictatorship was not opposed to democracy and was not a synonym for despotism because the ruling class considered democracy as appalling as dictatorship (if not more). After all, this conception survives in the ideas of 'elective dictatorship' and 'tyranny of the majority', which are still popular in British and American jurisprudence.[5]

So, dictatorship has been conceived *both* as the opposite of democracy *and* as an aspect of it. The reasons for this contradiction have been discussed by various theorists.[6] There are two main arguments put forward to explain this discrepancy. According to the first, the use of the concept to describe regimes and forms of exercise of public power is determined by political purposes. The meaning of the concept changes and follows the different historical modes of exercise of public power and class rule, reflecting the struggle between competing social forces. For instance, it has been argued that the identification of dictatorship with despotism and its opposition to democracy was consolidated in the process of the anti-Soviet campaign by the hegemonic states in the capitalist world.[7]

According to the second, the duality of meaning is inherent in the concept itself. There is a typology of dictatorship stemming from its original meaning in the Roman institution of *dictatura*. This refers to two types of dictatorship. On the one hand, there is the classical or original Roman dictatorship, which refers to an exceptional but constitutional institution whereby powers are conferred to a magistrate according to precisely defined procedures to deal with an emergency. The contemporary equivalent for this dictatorship would be the constitutional provision for a state of siege or a state of emergency. On the other hand, dictatorship refers to regimes whereby power has not been regularly

---

3 Ibid., 12.
4 Cortés, *Speech on Dictatorship*, 47.
5 See indicatively Basil S. Markesinis, 'Elective Dictatorship', 30 *Parliamentary Affairs*, 324; Jeremy Waldron, 'The Core of the Case against Judicial Review', 115 *Yale Law Journal* 1346.
6 See especially the works of Peter Baher and Melvin Richter (eds.), *Dictatorship in History and Theory: Bonapartism, Caesarism, and Totalitarianism* (Cambridge: Cambridge University Press, 2004); Draper, *The Dictatorship of the Proletariat*; Schmitt, *Dictatorship*.
7 Draper, *The Dictatorship of the Proletaria*, 7.

10 *Historical and theoretical foundations*

conferred and the legal order is overthrown rather than safeguarded.[8] The contemporary equivalent for this type of dictatorship would be any regime of arbitrary rule that was installed via an overthrow of the normal legal institutions.

This chapter begins the examination of the typologies of dictatorship while emphasising the socio-political context where they originated. The theme explored in this chapter is the claim by various theorists that there are two types of dictatorship and that there is an equivocal relationship between the two. The original argument pursued here is that this equivocal relationship is inevitable. The analysis will begin with the existing theoretical discussions of the Roman institution of dictatorship and continue with Carl Schmitt's dualism of commissarial and sovereign dictatorship.

Roman dictatorship

It can be argued that the existence of two types of dictatorship originated in ancient Rome. The *dictatura* was an important institution of the Roman Republic, but it came to signify two very different political realities. Initially, it referred to the exceptional magistracy that was legal and constitutional and was used roughly seventy-six times between 501 and 202 BC, before it vanished for 120 years. In 82 BC the institution of dictatorship was revived by Sulla and later by Julius Caesar, in the two most famous instances of dictatorship of the antiquity. However, this revival already brought the institution close to the modern meaning of dictatorship in the sense of a regime based on personal rule and power concentration. The former paradigm has been known as classical dictatorship and the latter as Caesaristic dictatorship. Therefore, the claim has been made that the discrepancy we identified above is due to the semantic slippage rooted in Roman history itself.[9]

To examine this claim, let us start by identifying the main features of the classical Roman dictatorship. First, it was constitutional and legal: there were precise circumstances that called for its invocation. On the one hand, was a series of precisely defined but uncommon duties (presiding over the Comitia in the absence of competent magistrates, performing the ancient propitiatory ritual of the *clavus annalis*, presiding over certain festivals, exceptional recruitment of the Senate, etc.);

---

8 See Baher and Richter, *Dictatorship in History and Theory*, 22; and Claude Nicolet, 'Dictatorship in Rome', in Baher and Richter (eds.), *Dictatorship in History and Theory*, 263.
9 Nicolet, *Dictatorship in Rome*, 275.

on the other hand, it would take form according to the formula, 'if a war or very substantial civil unrest arises', that is, in the event of a crisis of 'the common good'.[10] Thus, the second main characteristic of dictatorship is the specific mandate to provide for the common good. This is perhaps the most important characteristic, as the interpretation of what may promote the common good becomes determinant of the width or narrowness of the mandate. It is for this reason that the doctrine of the common good has been characterised as the 'last refuge of despotism'.[11] In the following sections I argue that the doctrine of the 'common good' is precisely the *locus of equivocation* (i.e. the gate that leads from the first to the second type of dictatorship).

The third characteristic of the classical dictatorship is its temporariness. Dictatorship lasted for a maximum of six months, but usually the dictator would hand his power back as soon as the specific task was accomplished. The dictator had to be nominated by one or both of the consuls. However, in 211 BC, on the advice of the Senate, the people were asked to elect a dictator, to some degree, directly.[12] This new element in the process of nomination signifies a change that foreshadowed the Caesaristic type of dictatorship that strongly relied on plebiscitarian representation. Julius Caesar's rule sought the support of the Italian public and of the urban plebs, through largesse (distributions, games, etc.), as well as through an elevation of the network of his clientele almost to the world scale. Nevertheless, his rule does not exhibit more advanced elements of plebiscitarianism of the type of 'consensus omnium' one encounters in Caesar Augustus's rule.[13] The last main feature of classical dictatorship, and arguably the distinguishing element between this and the Caesaristic type that emerged 120 years after its disappearance, was its limited nature: the dictatorship could not make new laws.[14] The dictator's jurisdiction was primarily military and not civil. Their mandate was to preserve the legal order and not to alter it. This is mainly the reason why classical dictatorship has been characterised not as a form of government in itself, but as an institutional component of a broader republican regime.[15]

---

10 Ibid., 265.
11 Ibid., 276.
12 Ibid., 267.
13 Ibid., 275.
14 Ibid., 266. See also Hal Draper, *Karl Marx's Theory of Revolution: Volume 3* (New York: Monthly Review Press, 1986), 12.
15 Andreas Kalyvas, 'The Tyranny of Dictatorship: When the Greek Tyrant Met the Roman Dictator', 35 *Political Theory*, 412, 417.

So if classical dictatorship is merely a component of a regime, Caesaristic dictatorship can be characterised as a type of regime. Sulla's dictatorship was the first example of this. According to Appian of Alexandria (95–165 AD), after his invasion of Rome in 82 BC, and following the death of the two consuls during the civil war, Sulla 'convinced' the Senate to appoint an interrex and subsequently 'persuaded' the interrex not to organise and supervise elections for new consuls but to appoint him dictator for an indefinite period and with legislative powers.[16] In the absence of consuls, the law that appointed Sulla was approved by the centuriate assembly. His mandate was provisional but was not strictly or temporally limited. His appointment as dictator *legibus scribundis et rei publicae constituendae* meant that he had the mandate to 'draw up laws and restore a constitution to the State'.

As a result, Sulla's dictatorship was a dictatorship for an indefinite period and with legislative powers. It is evident that two of the main characteristics of classical dictatorship have disappeared (i.e. the limited mandate to suspend the law without making new laws, as well as the temporal limitation). Nevertheless, the specific mandate that the dictator has to carry out (i.e. the mission for the common good) remains. Sulla's mandate as a dictator was to 'enact such laws as he himself might deem best and for the regulation of the Republic', 'until such time as he should firmly reestablish the City and Italy and the government in general'.[17]

On this basis, we can describe the relationship between classical and Caesaristic dictatorship in Rome as a unity in difference. Caesaristic dictatorship sheds two of the essential characteristics of classical dictatorship (i.e. the temporal limitation, as well as the exclusion of law-making powers) from the competence conferred on the dictator. It has been argued, however, that the constitutional principle of time limits 'does not indicate an essential difference between these two forms of power but rather an internal differentiation of degree'.[18] After all, even in the type of classical dictatorship, the six-month time limit seems arbitrary when a mandate is given for as general an objective as to provide for the common good. One could argue then that the characteristic common to both types, namely the specific mandate to provide for the common good (i.e. the *salus populi*, the safety or welfare of the people) is what leads to the abolition of the temporal limitation. A temporal limitation

---

16 Ibid., 424. See also Nicolet, *Dictatorship in Rome*, 269.
17 Frederik Juliaan Vervaet, 'The Lex Valeria and Sulla's Empowerment as Dictator (82–79 BCE)', in 15 *Cahiers du Centre Gustave Glot*, 37, 39–40.
18 Kalyvas, *The Tyranny of Dictatorship*, 425.

might eventually become an obstacle to the fulfilment of the mandate. Therefore, the main difference between classical and Caesaristic dictatorship is the conferral of law-making powers to the latter as opposed to the former.

Another argument that points to the unity of the two types involves assessing the social function of dictatorships. Thus, one would have to look at the content of the reforms that Sulla's dictatorship carried out, which would last until the end of the republic. Their goal was to reestablish the supremacy of the Senate in the Roman state, by requiring for instance that a bill acquired senatorial approval before it was submitted to the Tribunate (i.e. the plebeian council), by revoking the power of the tribunes to veto acts of the Senate, or by enacting a new treason law to prevent insurrection by provincial governor and army commanders.[19] The argument can be made that Sulla's dictatorship as a form of government reflected a specific balance of social forces and was instrumental in the struggle between the patricians (i.e. Rome's aristocracy) and the plebeians (i.e. Rome's popular classes). Sulla, belonging to the Optimates, the conservative political faction of ancient Rome, strongly opposed the popular agrarian reforms of the Gracchi, which sought to relieve the urban poor strata, thereby challenging the patrician class.

It was not just the revived dictatorship under Sulla that functioned as a political weapon in the struggle between social forces. The same was the case for the original institution of the Roman republic. Livy's historical account of the origins of dictatorship focuses on external factors. According to him, the appointment of a dictator for the first time, in 501 BC, by means of a *lex dictatore creando*, was due to the external dangers posed by the aggression of neighbouring tribes.[20] On the contrary, Dionysius's account stresses the central role played by domestic politics in the creation of the institution of dictatorship: the high polarisation in Roman society and the popular unrest due to the problem of debts and the civic discord between plebeians and patricians.[21] Following the enactment of a law proposed by the consul Publius Valerius (*Publicola*), which strengthened considerably the position of the plebeians by granting the right to appeal (*ius provocationis*) to Roman citizens, proposing that no Roman should be punished without a trial,[22] the Senate

---

19 Frank Frost Abbott, *A History and Description of Roman Political Institutions* (London: Elibron Classics, 1901) 103.
20 Kalyvas, *The Tyranny of Dictatorship*, 415.
21 Ibid., 419.
22 Ibid.

proposed the creation of a new magistracy 'endowed with authority over war and peace and every other matter, possessed of absolute power and subject to no accounting for either its counsels or its actions'.[23]

We conclude that the institution of dictatorship was deliberately designed to suppress the political ambition of the plebeians. It was an aristocratic political instrument aimed at turmoil and preserving the interests of patricians by ensuring that the exercise of their class rule would not be hindered by formal procedures, such as the *ius provocationis*. Here, another fundamental characteristic of the institution of dictatorship comes to the surface (i.e. the militarisation of political contestation). The institution of dictatorship abolished the distinction between the *imperium domi* (i.e. the power exercised within the city that was limited and circumscribed by various institutional checks) and the *imperium militia* (i.e. the power exercised outside the confines of the city).[24] From then on, in case of a 'very substantial civil unrest', the *imperium militiae* could be brought inside the city and restore order, thus, reproducing the rule of the dominant class. The political adversary turned into a *hostis* (i.e. a public enemy), foreshadowing a central function of dictatorial regimes in the twentieth century. And when the need arose for the powers conferred to include the power to alter the law and constitution, the idea of dictatorship came to signify a new type of regime—the Caesaristic dictatorship.

Commissarial and sovereign dictatorship

So far we have established that, based on the readings of the Roman institution of dictatorship, a typology of dictatorship is formed. Two types of dictatorship emerge: one is an essential institution of the republic and resembles the modern institution of state of siege or state of emergency; and the other is a form of government that resembles the modern dictatorial regimes. The distinguishing element between these two is the conferral of law-making powers (i.e. powers that alter and not merely safeguard the existing legal order). If the discussion of the Roman institution provides us with a view of the historical origins of dictatorship, I want to proceed now with Carl Schmitt's elaboration on the concept, which I believe presents in a concise manner its main elements and dualistic nature, and can help sketch out its theoretical foundations as well as its inherent contradictions.

---

23 Ibid., 420.
24 Benedetto Fontana, 'The Concept of Caesarism in Gramsci', in Baher and Richter (eds.), *Dictatorship in History and Theory*, 187.

Schmitt defines 'dictatorship' in the 1926 'Staatslexikon im Auftrage der Görresgesellschaft' as 'the exercise of state power freed from any legal restrictions, for the purpose of resolving an abnormal situation—in particular, a situation of war and rebellion'.[25] According to Schmitt, the concept of dictatorship consists of two decisive elements:

> on the one hand the idea of a normal situation that a dictatorship restores or establishes, and on the other the idea that, in the event of an abnormal situation, certain legal barriers are suspended in favour of resolving this situation through dictatorship.[26]

There are two issues that can be raised with regards to this definition. First, the central presence of an idea of normality whose restoration must be prioritised. A mechanism for the resolution of abnormal situations is essential for a system of rule to reproduce itself. What is more, the questions 'what is normal?', as well as 'what is necessary to restore this normality?', are crucial for the issue of dictatorship and especially for its function in the context of social struggle. The second issue relates to the form of exercise of state power specific to dictatorship, which consists in the suspension of legal barriers. Dictatorship reveals the relationship between law and violence, but not violence for violence's sake; rather, a violence exerted for a specific purpose (i.e. safeguarding a legal order). This point has far-reaching consequences when it comes to discussing dictatorship's relation to the law. If dictatorship is exercise of state power freed from any legal restrictions, then one can argue that law poses a limit to state power *only to the extent that state power is not necessary* to intervene to ensure the reproduction of a legal order. The limits that law poses on state power are themselves inherently limited by a fundamental necessity that underlies both law and dictatorship, norm and exception—namely, the necessity of reproduction.

Schmitt's 1926 definition is based on the typology he had developed in his 1921 book, *Dictatorship*. There, he distinguishes between two types of dictatorship, a commissarial dictatorship and a sovereign dictatorship. The commissarial dictatorship corresponds to the type of classical Roman dictatorship discussed above: it is a republican institution, temporally limited in its exercise during emergency circumstances by a specified commissarial mandate to restore the previously standing legal

---

25 Schmitt, *Dictatorship*, xxiii.
26 Ibid.

order.[27] Despite its extra-legal authorisation, this institution remains within the prescriptions of a constitutional order in which the dictator is constitutionally mandated.[28] On the other hand, a sovereign dictatorship is unlimited in its parameters and may proceed to establish a completely new order.[29] This type of dictatorship corresponds to the dictatorships of Sulla and Caesar, whereby emergency powers were used to change the constitutional order of Rome. Nevertheless, it is not until the development of the modern bourgeois states and the modern notion of sovereignty that accompanied this that the notion of sovereign dictatorship achieves its full meaning. For Schmitt, a sovereign dictatorship 'is exercised by a national assembly that has at its disposal state power without legal limitations when the existing constitutional order has been abolished—say, after a revolution—and the new constitution has not yet been implemented'.[30] The revival of the notion of dictatorship following the French Revolution and the consolidation of bourgeois power is connected, according to Schmitt, with the process of secularisation of the source of authority, as the exercise of public power that was theretofore divinely sanctioned had to be thereafter popularly legitimated.

As was the case with the classical and Caesaristic types of Roman dictatorship, the main difference between commissarial and sovereign dictatorship is the conferral of law/constitution-making powers. Both Schmittian types of dictatorship share the features of permanence and specific mandate. However, this statement has to be qualified for it is inherently contradictory. According to Schmitt, both commissarial and sovereign dictatorships function on the basis of a mandate. The commissarial dictator will operate within the 'limits' set out by law to protect the legal order 'in the name of the people'. Similarly, the sovereign dictator will legislate so as to constitute a new legal order, again 'in the name of the people'. But the similarity of the existence of a mandate in both types of dictatorship pales in comparison to the difference in the degree of these mandates. The specificity of a commissarial mandate to wage war or to suppress a rebellion is compared to a mandate so general that it arguably goes necessarily beyond the limits of any mandate and any temporal restriction. One mandate is to restore an existing

---

27 John P. McCormick, 'From Constitutional Technique to Caesarist Ploy: Carl Schmitt on Dictatorship, Liberalism, and Emergency Powers', in Baher and Richter (eds.), *Dictatorship in History and Theory*, 197–198.
28 Schmitt, *Dictatorship*, xxiv.
29 McCormick, *From Constitutional Technique*, 197–198.
30 Schmitt, *Dictatorship*, xxiv.

normality, whereas the other is to establish a new one. Despite the possible equivocation between old and new normalities, the far-reaching nature of the sovereign mandate cannot be contested.

With regards to the feature of permanence and transitionality, contradictions are apparent here too. In his 'Dictatorship', Schmitt discusses Bodin. He says that, for Bodin, Roman dictators were definitely not sovereign, as they only had one mandate, such as to wage war, to suppress uproar, to reform the state or to manage the new organisation of offices. Not even the Decemviri, who had complete authority to introduce a new constitution can be called sovereign in the proper sense, because their power ceased with the completion of the mandate.[31] With this point Schmitt attempts to draw a line on the blurred distinction between sovereignty and sovereign dictatorship. He argues that power is not sovereign when it is not permanent. The Decemviri, with their far-reaching mandate (i.e. to introduce a new constitution), are an example of sovereign dictatorship because their power is temporally limited. Their rule is transitional.

Permanence is a trait of sovereignty, whereas temporariness is a trait of dictatorship. This statement is not uncontroversial. If dictatorship is always transitional, how is one to characterise regimes such as Sulla's, Caesar's, Cromwell's or Bonaparte's? What is the temporal limit of such regimes? Where does 'sovereign dictatorship' end, and when does it give its place to the 'new normality'? Schmitt uses the example of the French Revolution to tackle these rising contradictions. The National Convention assembled on 20 September 1792 is the example of a 'sovereign dictator' given by Schmitt. After the Convention drafted the constitution of 24 June 1793 and the people accepted it in a general election, its mandate was concluded. However, because the state of external war and internal counter-revolution threatened the constitution, the Convention decided on 10 October 1793 that the provisional government of France should be a revolutionary one until peace had been established. Therefore, the constitution of 1793 was suspended. But the constitution itself provided for no constituted organ to declare the suspension. Consequently, according to Schmitt, the Convention acted through a direct appeal to the constituent power of the people, in which it simultaneously claimed that it was inhibited in its exercise by the war and by the counter-revolution.[32]

The most common answer to the question, 'which institution can be defined as dictatorial during the French Revolution?', would probably

31 Ibid., 20.
32 Ibid., 127–128.

be the Committee of Public Safety—even more likely, it would be just its leader, Robespierre, that would be defined as a dictator. But, for Schmitt, however powerful the Comité de salut public became over the years, 'legally there was no doubt that it was only active on behalf of the Committee of the National Convention, and on its mandate'.[33] The Committee of Public Safety could perhaps be described, using the Schmittian typology, as a commissary dictatorship within the framework of the sovereign dictatorship of the National Convention. However, for Schmitt, neither institution had any intention of awarding itself a degree of permanence. For this reason they would represent different types of dictatorship.

Based on the above, we could argue that Schmitt conceives of sovereign dictatorship as something different from Caesaristic dictatorship. Sovereign dictatorship does not refer to a type of regime. Permanence is not its feature. It may be used to describe transitional situations where a non-constituted organ (following a revolution or a coup d'état) constitutes a new legal order using plenary law-making powers. Sovereign dictatorship is a combination of the transitional element of classical, commissarial dictatorial powers with general law-making powers. This is why Schmitt elaborates on the relationship between the legislator (right devoid of legal power) and the dictator (omnipotence without law) to illustrate the nature of sovereign dictatorship.

> When a relationship emerges that makes it possible to give the legislator the power of a dictator, to create a dictatorial legislator and constitutional dictator, then the commissary dictatorship has become a sovereign dictatorship. This relationship will come about through an idea that is, in its substance, a consequence of Rousseau's Contrat social, although he does not name as a separate power: le pouvoir constituant [the constituting power].[34]

Several points might be raised in relation to the above passage. First, the relationship between dictatorship and the law is always there and never questioned in both types of dictatorship. On the one hand, in commissary dictatorship, it is the exercise of power unrestrained from law that safeguards law itself. The mandate stems from an existing constitution. On the other hand, sovereign dictatorship does not deal with sheer power because this power is associated with the constitution as foundational to it. Sovereign dictatorship does not appeal to

33 Ibid., 130.
34 Ibid., 110–111.

an existing constitution, but to one that is still to come. This is why the concept of constituent power of the people is crucial here; because the people as carrier of this power relate it to the constitution-to-come as foundational to it.

This brings us to the second issue of the dictatorship and the concept of the people. Both forms of dictatorship are based on the idea of the sovereign people. But, whereas in commissarial dictatorship the deputies of the people, acting within the already constituted order, seek to preserve this order by suspending certain legal provisions, in sovereign dictatorship the people's role as a legislator and as a dictator coincides to found a new constitution. The exercise of constituent power in the name of the people is the distinguishing element of sovereign dictatorship. However, both types of dictatorship are legitimated by the notion of the people.

Still, the contradictions of Schmitt's sovereign dictatorship are not entirely resolved. We saw above that, for Schmitt, sovereign dictatorship is different from Caesaristic dictatorship due to the former's transitional nature. However, it has been argued that, in the context Schmitt was writing, the spirit of sovereign dictatorship of the French Revolution was embodied by the Soviet power.[35] For Schmitt, the Marxist understanding of dictatorship, captured in the concept of the dictatorship of the proletariat, re-focuses on the element of transitionality and the commissarial character of the idea of dictatorship. For the communists, 'dictatorship is just a means to reach a certain goal, because its content is only determined by the interest of the intended outcome'; the dictatorship of the proletariat is 'just a technical means to achieve the communists' final goal'.[36] The problem here is whether the dictatorship of the proletariat can be accurately construed under the notion of sovereign dictatorship. Would the whole historical experience of the Soviet regime be described as a sovereign dictatorship? If not, which exact periods could be described as such? Would it only signify the period from the October Revolution until the first Constitution of the Russian Socialist Federated Soviet Republic of July 1918? If so, then sovereign dictatorship seems to describe processes entirely different than the ones described by the concept of dictatorship of the proletariat.

To make more sense of these issues, it is important to look at the socio-political context in which Schmitt developed his typology of dictatorship and understand the political instrumentality of his theory. In the context of intensified political and ideological struggle, the main

---

35 McCormick, *From Constitutional Technique*, 200–202.
36 Schmitt, *Dictatorship*, xi.

question that troubled Schmitt from a bourgeois standpoint was the potentially unlimited competence of a sovereign dictatorship that is legitimated and bound by a future situation. According to Schmitt, the communist dictatorship represented the culmination of the modern historical trend toward totally unrestrained political action.[37] Schmitt was an eye-witness to the establishment of the Soviet Republic of Munich and Southern Bavaria. The Free Corps forces under Johannes Hoffmann (the elected Bavarian minister) and Gustav Noske (the German minister of defence) had descended quickly upon Bavaria, and Munich in particular, to counter the communist threat. The consideration of establishing a military dictatorship with Noske at its head arguably influenced Schmitt's elaborations on the notion.

One could then argue that there is a certain political instrumentality at play in Schmitt's typology of dictatorship. Schmitt attacks left-wing sovereign dictatorship, whose spirit is embodied in the revolutionary movement of 1789 and carried forward in 1848 and 1917 by the proletariat, as potentially unlimited and, therefore, as a distortion of the original commissarial character of dictatorship. For the same reasons and following the same line of reasoning, he defends commissarial dictatorship because it seeks to reproduce the existing legal order (and class balance) using a strict and temporally limited mandate. Consequently, Schmitt's goal is not just to make a theoretical contribution that unmasks the deficiency of bourgeois literature on the subject of dictatorship, but also to render the communist use of the term illegitimate, while offering a more legitimate, constitutional, commissarial alternative that the bourgeois state (and ruling class) could use to reproduce its existence.[38]

This argument, based on the political instrumentality of Schmitt's theoretical work, has been furthered to analyse most of his works during the interwar period.[39] For instance, it has been argued that towards the end of *Dictatorship* and in his following works, Schmitt seems to develop the view that perhaps a commissarial dictatorship is not enough to confront the communist sovereign dictatorship. For this, a countertheory of right-wing sovereign dictatorship is needed.[40] In his next book, *Political Theology,* Schmitt advances the fusion of sovereignty

---

37 McCormick, *From Constitutional Technique*, 199.
38 Ibid., 200–201.
39 Ibid. See also W.E. Scheuerman, *Carl Schmitt: The End of Law* (London: Rowman & Littlefield, 1999) as well as Renato Cristi, *Carl Schmitt and Authoritarian Liberalism: Strong State, Free Economy* (Cardiff: University of Wales Press, 1998).
40 Ibid., 201.

Historical and theoretical foundations 21

and emergency powers. Sovereignty is embodied in the President of the Reich who is not encumbered by constitutional restraints but only by the demands of the political contingency, because the exception cannot be circumscribed factually and made to conform to a preformed law. Schmitt's fusion of sovereignty and dictatorship in *Political Theology* seems to provide bourgeois theory of the interwar period with a counter-notion of dictatorship that is as all-encompassing and constitutionally abrogating as that of the communists.[41]

By 1931 and his *The Guardian of the Constitution*, Schmitt's proposal was more clearly elaborated. Schmitt was openly attacking what he saw as an inefficient liberal Rechstaat, incapable of making a political decision on the friend and the enemy of the regime—a prerequisite for dealing with the communist threat. Only a dictatorship of the nation embodied in the President is capable of countering the communist threat of a 'sovereign' dictatorship of the proletariat. The formulations in *The Guardian* are not so far from Schmitt's 1933 work celebrating the Nazi regime. The President's authority, binding itself immediately with the political total will of the people, foreshadows the Führer's leadership principle of the Nazi regime. By 1933 the identity of the Führer with the nation's will, expressed in the plebiscitary immediacy of the deciding people as legislator, had replaced the President's representative relation with the nation.[42] Continuity is evident here. Schmitt's theory clearly articulates the unity of the German people, unmediated through social-group organisations, as prerequisite for the unmediated expression of the general will, mirroring Rousseau's classical exposition.[43] It is important to note that Schmitt's elaborations that point towards a dictatorial solution do not lie at the margins but at the core of bourgeois juridico-political theory. They manifest the reactionary potential of the formal bourgeois conception of democracy, whereby a sovereign dictatorship can be called in the name of the people and democracy.

Perhaps the most important point to grasp here is the reason why Schmitt argues in favour of a right-wing sovereign dictatorship rather than a commissarial one to counter the communist threat. We established above that the distinguishing element of sovereign dictatorship is the power to alter the constitution to achieve the necessary end. The particular socio-economic and political situation of interwar Germany called for such far-reaching structural transformation in the

---

41 Ibid., 202.
42 See Carl Schmitt, *State, Movement, People* (Corvallis: Plutarch Press, 2001).
43 Jean-Jacques Rousseau, *The Social Contract* (Oxford: Oxford University Press, 2008), 66.

macroeconomic, social and political fields that could not be achieved within the temporal and task-bound limits of commissarial dictatorship. This is a key point to understand the contradictions between the two kinds of dictatorship and the difficulty of characterising historical examples as one or the other, or identifying the exact historical point when one turns into the other. It is essential to grasp that it is the reproduction of a regime of power, property and production relations—disguised in such concepts as common good, *salus populi* or general interest—that dictates the extent of alteration necessary to restore normality. To the extent that an existential threat to the reproduction of the bourgeois state and bourgeois rule cannot be dealt with unless the legal framework for the exercise of public power is changed, the commissarial dictatorship (of a state of emergency provision) will necessarily be replaced by a sovereign dictatorship. Schmitt's sovereign dictatorship appears thus as a prerequisite for Caesaristic dictatorship. A constitutional change is necessary for the reproduction of a system of social relations by a dictatorial regime. The following chapters explore the historical tendencies that have necessitated and may necessitate such change in the future.

Despite the evident political motivation behind Schmitt's typology of dictatorship, one cannot disregard the analytically interesting aspects of this typology. It certainly captures an essential aspect that differentiates the classical Roman type of dictatorship from the modern notion of dictatorship: the power to alter the constitution. It establishes analytically interesting (albeit not uncontroversial) lines of demarcation between the types of commissarial, sovereign and Caesaristic dictatorship and leads to useful conclusions about the contradictions and commonalities of these types and the reasons why one may turn into the other. However, as we saw above, it definitely fails to accurately conceive of and describe the Marxist concept of dictatorship.

Exception, emergency, necessity

The commissarial dictatorship is mostly associated today with the institution of a state of siege, or state of exception, state of emergency or state of necessity. These terms are often used interchangeably, but I believe it is pertinent here to examine the different nuance between them. We saw above that after *Dictatorship*, Schmitt develops his theory of sovereignty as part of a theory of the state of exception. The exception is the locus of sovereignty, for Schmitt, because the decision to suspend the entire existing order is a decision of unlimited authority that serves an existential purpose for the bourgeois state. In such a situation the state remains, whereas the law recedes.[44]

The other major exponent of the term 'state of exception' is Giorgio Agamben. His analysis of the state of exception is based on Schmitt's famous statement that 'sovereign is he who decides on the exception'. Agamben builds on Schmitt's analysis to examine the relation between law and exception, in what he calls the paradox of sovereignty. For Agamben, the paradox of sovereignty consists in the sovereign being, at the same time, outside and inside.[45] The sovereign, having the legal power to suspend the validity of the law, legally places themselves outside the law. 'According to its etymological root, the exception is truly taken outside (ex-capere), and not simply excluded'.[46]

It makes sense, thus, for Agamben to use the term state of exception on the grounds that exception connotes being 'taken outside'.[47] Moreover, this state of exception has by now become the rule, resulting, thus, in a new form of government, which knows no law and is bound by no law. This form of government is particularly evident after 9/11 and is captured in the idea of the camp, an example of which is the legal blackhole of Guantanamo Bay. This argument is furthered in Agamben's critique of the security state. Agamben saw the extension of the state of emergency in France, following the Paris attacks of 2015, as a further step in the radical transformation of the liberal state. So, even though Agamben uses the term 'security state' more than the term 'state of exception', it is evident that the latter is the specific characteristic of the former.

The crux of Agamben's argument is that the state of exception is not a dictatorship but 'a space devoid of law, a zone of anomie in which all legal determinations—and above all the very distinction between public and private—are deactivated'.[48] For him, 'all those theories that seek to annex the state of exception immediately to the law are

---

44 Carl Schmitt, *Political Theology Four Chapters on the Concept of Sovereignty* (Chicago: University of Chicago Press, 2004), 12.
45 Giorgio Agamben, *Homo Sacer: Sovereign Power and Bare Life* (Stanford: Stanford University Press, 1998), 15.
46 Ibid., 18.
47 Schmitt himself had opted to talk of the state of exception, rather than emergency, on the grounds that not all states of emergency constitute a threat to the norm or a challenge to sovereignty (for instance, states of emergency called on the grounds of 'natural' catastrophes).
48 Giorgio Agamben, *State of Exception* (Chicago: University of Chicago Press, 2005), 50.

false'.[49] To develop this argument, Agamben uses the Roman institution of *iustitium*, instead of the Roman *dictatura*, as archetype of the state of exception. The *iustitium* was used in situations that endangered the Republic, whereby

> the Senate would issue a senatus consultum ultimum (final decree of the Senate) by which it called upon the consuls and, in some cases, the praetor and the tribunes of the people, and even, in extreme cases, all citizens, to take whatever measures they considered necessary for the salvation of the state.[50]

The institution did not entail the creation of a new magistracy, but rather the investment of every citizen with 'a floating and anomalous imperium that resists definition within the terms of the normal order'.[51]

Agamben argues that the *iustitium* cannot be interpreted through the paradigm of dictatorship. The latter conferred an imperium that was extremely broad to a dictator chosen by the consuls, whereas the former suspended the laws that restricted the action of existing magistrates, who would enjoy unlimited power following the *iustitium*.[52] Under this prism, the state of exception is not defined as a conferral of plenary powers, but as 'a kenomatic state, an emptiness and standstill of the law'.[53] Agamben uses one historical example of this institution to illustrate this point. He cites Theodor Mommsen's description of 'the case of a private citizen, Scipio Nasica, who, when confronted with the consul's refusal to act against Tiberius Gracchus in execution of a senatus consultum ultimum, exclaims, "He who wishes that the state be safe, let him follow me!"'.[54] According to Agamben, in killing Tiberius Gracchus, Scipio Nasica acted 'as if he were a consul', transforming this call to an investment of any and every citizen with a power that is floating and 'outside of the law'.

It has to be noted, though, that this is a rather problematic example to illustrate the institution of the *iustitium*. Scipio Nasica was not just any private citizen. He was a senator (in fact he was the *pontifex maximus*, i.e. chief pontiff and princeps senates, i.e. leader of the Senate) who opposed the policies promoted in the Tribune by Tiberius Gracchus, policies of reform that aimed to ameliorate the conditions of the plebs

---

49 Ibid.
50 Ibid., 41.
51 Ibid., 43.
52 Ibid., 47.
53 Ibid., 48.
54 Ibid., 44–45.

at the expense of the patrician interests, and thus the interests of Scipio Nasica. However, it seems that he was not authorised by any legal institution to kill Tiberius Gracchus. There is nothing in the descriptions of either Cicero[55] or Plutarch[56] that supports the view that Tiberius Gracchus's murder was carried out under the authority of a *iustitium* or any other institution.

It seems that Agamben is impressed by the fact that every citizen is potentially invested with an imperium to safeguard the city and resolve the situation of danger, as well as the fact that this institution does not confer extra powers, but merely suspends the law, so that possibly anyone can 'save' the law and the city. However, his argument is problematic because there does not seem to be any historical evidence for the exercise of emergency powers by the whole citizenry. Even more problematic is the fact that he tries to elevate this institution to a paradigm that can help explain modern juridico-political forms, by isolating certain elements of this institution and ignoring others.

It should not be forgotten that Agamben uses the above example so as to strengthen his argument on the complete separation of the state of exception from the rule of law. This separation comes under criticism by Mark Neocleous. Neocleous argues (based on historical evidence gathered from the U.K., the U.S.A., Israel, South Africa and Latin American countries) that emergency powers are far from exceptional; rather, they are an ongoing aspect of normal political rule and have been crucial to the consolidation of capitalist modernity. To criticise, as Agamben does, the use of emergency powers in terms of a suspension of the law is to make the mistake of counterpoising normality and emergency, law and violence. Neocleous opposes this rigid separation as well as the idea of the 'permanent state of exception' that stems from it.

For this reason, he opts for the term state of emergency instead of state of exception, since the state of emergency is what emerges from the rule of law when violence needs to be exercised and the limits of the rule of law overcome. 'Far from being outside the rule of law, emergency powers emerge from within it. They are thus as important as the rule of law to the political management of the modern state'.[57] In this manner, Neocleous's state of emergency reveals the unity of law and

---

55 Cicero, *Cicero on the Emotions: Tusculan Disputations 3 and 4* (Chicago: University of Chicago Press, 2002), 57.
56 Plutarch, *Plutarch's Lives: Vol. X, The Life of Tiberius Gracchus* (London: William Heinemann, 1959), 189–191.
57 Mark Neocleous, 'The Problem with Normality: Taking Exception to "Permanent Emergency"', 31 *Alternatives: Global, Local, Political*, 191.

exception. 'Emergency powers do not involve some kind of suspension of law while violence takes place, but are united with law for the exercise of a violence necessary for the permanent refashioning of order'.[58]

Furthermore, this unity of law and exception points towards the socio-economic content that determines these different forms. The fact that every constitution contains provisions for emergency rule leads to the conclusion that 'the ruling class was never going to be so stupid as to produce a constitution that does not allow it to suspend fundamental liberties and rights in the name of emergency'.[59] There is, one could argue, a fundamental need of the ruling class that is served by the existence of constitutional emergency powers. The institution of emergency powers, therefore, objectively functions to reproduce a regime of power relations that safeguard specific social interests.

Therefore, to reduce the resistance to emergency measures to a return to legality and the rule of law, Neocleous argues, is based on the illusion that law has a life of its own. The rigid separation of law and exception can be as harmful for a critical analysis of the public legal form as the analysis that reduces one to the other without taking into account of the differences and nuances between the two. Consequently, it is important to further Neocleous's argument against 'abstracting the rule of law from its origins in class domination and oppression', while showing, at the same time, what necessitates this change in form.

In doing so, it is pertinent to examine yet another term used to characterise the emergency legislation, namely the state of necessity. Agamben himself criticises the view that posits the concept of necessity at the foundation of the state of exception. According to him, 'necessity is not a source of law, nor does it properly suspend the law; it merely releases a particular case from the literal application of the norm'.[60] He argues that the ultimate ground of the exception is not necessity, but the principle according to which 'every law is ordained for the common well-being of men'. So, for Agamben, the state of exception suspends the juridical order as such, as it is based on the *salus populi*, whereas with necessity it is a question of a particular case.

Contrary to Agamben, it has been argued that necessity operates on a plane beneath both norm and exception: a plane that determines whether law is enough (and whether a commissarial or a sovereign exceptional regime is necessary) to deal with an existential crisis of the state. Normality and exception are underlined by the same fundamental

---

58 Ibid.
59 Ibid.
60 Agamben, *State of Exception*, 25.

necessity, which gives birth to different forms of exercise of public power. The analysis of the continuity between normality and crisis-exception, which the concept of necessity captures, may be attributed to Kantorowicz.[61] Kantorowicz reveals the inextricable link between necessity and law, and the way in which an exceptional situation turns into a new normality, in the example of taxation: how it turned from exceptional to constant necessity, a *perpetua necessitas*. Necessity may not be a legal rule itself, but it lies within the rule. The concept of necessity enables the conceptualisation of the unity between norm and exception, as well as the common function of these forms in reproducing not only the power of the state but also a specific regime of property and production relations.

This modern conception of necessity can be traced back even further to the Roman concept of *salus populi*. The Roman maxim of *salus populi suprema lex esto* appears in Cicero's 'De Legibus' as the Roman equivalent of the welfare of the people, the general welfare, or the general interest. The general welfare becomes the supreme law (i.e. arguably the source of all law) and may be used to justify the suspension of law.

The strong influence that Roman juridico-political thought had on political theorists of the early modernity is evidenced in the way in which *salus populi* features in the juridico-political theories of Thomas Hobbes and John Locke. In their work, the material content of necessity is manifested, as private property is shown to be a precondition of the *salus populi* and a just society. For instance, John Locke in his 'Second Treatise of Government' outlines the relationship between the office of the sovereign, the institution of property and the *salus populi*. He recognises that in a constituted commonwealth there can be 'but one supreme power, which is the legislative'.[62] However, this legislative power is only a fiduciary power to act for certain ends; 'there remains still in the people a supreme power to remove or alter the legislative, when they find the legislative act contrary to the trust reposed in them' to attain this end.[63] According to Locke, the end to be achieved by the office of the sovereign is the 'welfare of the people': 'salus populi suprema lex, is certainly so just and fundamental a rule, that he, who sincerely follows it, cannot dangerously err'.[64]

---

61 Ernst Kantorowicz, *The King's Two Bodies: A Study in Mediaeval Political Theology* (New Jersey: Princeton University Press, 1997), 284–285.
62 John Locke, *Two Treatises of Government* (Cambridge: Cambridge University Press, 2012), 366.
63 Ibid.
64 Ibid., 373.

The protection of the *salus populi* is the fundamental necessity of a system of justice, and legislating for the 'common good' is the criterion of a good government. Therefore, 'whatsoever shall be done manifestly for the good of the people . . . is, and always will be, just prerogative.[65] Additionally, for Locke, as well as for Hobbes, the 'general interest' consists not just in the 'safety' of the person of all individuals, but more importantly in the protection of their property. For Hobbes, *salus populi* means not just 'a bare preservation, but also other contentments of life, which every man by lawful industry, . . . shall acquire to himself'.[66] Likewise, for Locke,

> the reason why men enter into society, is the preservation of their property; and the end why they choose and authorize a legislative, is, that there may be laws made, and rules set, as guards and fences to the properties of all the members of the society.[67]

The following chapters further elaborate on the concept of *salus populi* and its significance not just for the dictatorial form but for every bourgeois juridico-political form. This concept, central to the notion and institution of dictatorship, essentially points towards the potentially dictatorial character of every form of the bourgeois state.

---

65 Ibid.
66 Thomas Hobbes, *Leviathan* (Oxford: Oxford University Press, 2008), 222.
67 John Locke, *Two Treatises of Government*, 412.

2 Dictatorship and consolidation of bourgeois power

Modern dictatorship

We saw above that the Roman institution of dictatorship was not used for 120 years, between 501 BC and 81 BC, only to reappear in a different form in the context of intensified contradictions (between the patricians and plebeians). It is not surprising then that the re-emergence of the concept and institution in the eighteenth century posed new challenges to understanding its meaning. However, it may seem surprising that the institution vanished for so long. Why did it vanish and why did it re-emerge after so many centuries?

The re-emergence of dictatorship in the late eighteenth century followed the first instances of power centralisation, resulting from the bourgeois revolutions and the accompanying process, taking place in the field of political ideas and constitutional theory, of undermining the divine sources of authority. The rediscovery and use of Roman categories and institutions following the ascendancy of the bourgeois class is well documented. In the field of private law, revisiting the Roman institutions of private property, contract and legal personhood, as well as the concepts accompanying them, was necessary for the establishment and consolidation of capitalist social relations.[1] Karl Marx identified the use of Roman categories by the leaders, parties and masses of the French Revolution as essential for the task of 'unchaining and setting up modern bourgeois society'.[2]

The rise to power of the bourgeois class and the consolidation of its rule were accompanied by the process of secularisation of the source of

---

1 Michael E. Tigar and Madeleine R. Levy, *Law and the Rise of Capitalism* (New York: Monthly Review Press, 1977).
2 Karl Marx, 'The Eighteenth Brumaire of Louis Bonaparte', in Karl Marx and Friedrich Engels, *Collected Works: Volume 11* (London: Lawrence and Wishart, 2010), 105.

authority of its regime. Their struggle against the divinely sanctioned, hierarchical social relations of feudalism, which had for centuries resulted in a system of special rules applying to individuals of a certain status, meant that the new bourgeois regimes had to seek a different source of authority. A result of this process was the development of theories of social contract and popular sovereignty. The establishment of the people as source of authority meant that institutions of the Roman Republic could be revisited for inspiration in the field of public law. Dictatorship, as the exemplary Roman institution that protected the *salus populi* while safeguarding the legal order and reproducing state power, would have been an essential aspect of this process.

The importance of the issue of the source of authority for the re-emergence of the concept of dictatorship in modernity was highlighted by Carl Schmitt, who is well known for his insight into the genealogy of the central terminology of public law.[3] According to Schmitt,

> the sixteenth and seventeenth centuries were less interested in the development that led from democracy to Caesarism, because the absolute monarchy that emerged at that time did not find its legitimation in any consensus of the people, but saw itself as legitimised through God's grace.[4]

Expanding this statement, one could argue that the popular legitimation of a regime meant that an interest in historical developments concerning the crises of democratic regimes was bound to develop.

Schmitt's analysis of the National Convention as the exemplary institution of sovereign dictatorship in the context of the French Revolution confirms this point, but here I want to focus on another institution that could be characterised as having wielded dictatorial powers during the French Revolution, namely, the Committee of Public Safety (Comité de salut public). We can start by noticing the name of the Committee. This includes the concept that serves as guiding principle of the institution of dictatorship (i.e. the *salus populi*). It was set up by a decree of the National Convention on 6 April 1793, and broad supervisory powers over military as well as judicial efforts were conferred upon it with the goal of protecting the nascent Republic against foreign attacks and internal counter-revolution. According to Article 2 of the decree, its mandate was 'to supervise and accelerate the action of the provisional executive council, whose decisions it [could] even suspend when it

---

3 See Schmitt, *Political Theology*.
4 Schmitt, *Dictatorship*, 2.

[considered] them contrary to the national interest'. Article 7 established the Committee for one month, making it an example of a commissarial dictatorship in Schmittian terms. However, its mandate was extended and it became the *de facto* executive branch of government until the Constitution of 1795, which abolished it and established the Directory as the new institution of the executive.

One could argue that in Schmittian terms the institutions of the National Convention and the Committee of Public Safety were the first modern examples of a 'sovereign' and a 'commissarial dictatorship', respectively. The Law of 14 Frimaire II (4 December 1793) established the National Convention as the unique pulsing centre of the government and contributed greatly towards the centralisation of the administrative function. Article 2 of Section II placed all agencies and civil servants under the control of the Committee of Public Safety, while article 3 explicitly provided that surveillance was a part of the execution of the laws. The duties of surveillance were transferred to national agents, who were appointed and monitored by the Committees (Section II, Articles 14–16).[5] Last but not least, article 1 of Section IV authorised the Committee of Public Safety to take all necessary measures to change the organisation of the constituted authorities, while article 2 imposed on the people's representatives the responsibility to complete without delay the thorough purification of all the constituted authorities.

The Reign of Terror started as a war measure, a commissarial dictatorship introduced by the sovereign dictatorship of the National Convention. After the war measures became superfluous with the victory at Fleurus against the foreign enemy, this regime remained essential for the factional group of the bourgeois class led by Robespierre, which saw the revolutionary wing led by the Commune of Paris as a danger to its power.[6] The Reign of Terror during the French Revolution can be characterised as a dictatorial regime, combining elements of sovereign and commissarial dictatorship—to use Schmittian terms—so as to establish the nascent bourgeois Republic and protect it against foreign enemies and internal counter-revolution. Furthermore, according to Schmitt, this regime and measures like the institution of the commissars of revolution of the National Convention, who were externally omnipotent but internally dependent, were manifestations of the processes of centralisation of power and bureaucratisation that were then perfected by the Bonapartist regimes.[7]

5 Ibid., 143–144.
6 Draper, *Karl Marx's Theory of Revolution*, 365.
7 Schmitt, *Dictatorship*, 145.

Before we move on to discuss the relationship between dictatorship and Bonapartism, I want to examine another historical event that came to be characterised as a dictatorship—General Cavaignac's state of siege, which dealt with the revolutionary threat posed by the French proletariat in 1848. In the 'June days' of 1848, when the Paris working class erupted in revolt following the pan-European revolutionary wave, the provisional government replied by proclaiming a state of siege and investing General Cavaignac with the authority to quell the rebellion. The term dictatorship was not used officially, but was common in the press and on everyone's tongue.[8]

Cavaignac assumed powers first on 24 June following a proclamation; however, he demanded to be reinvested with the same authority by a normal act of the Assembly following mature deliberation. This took place on 28 June, when he went through the motions of 'laying down his powers' and the deputies 'made not the least pretence of mature deliberation in scrambling to give them back'.[9] The state of siege had no temporal limitations and resulted in 'three thousands of the insurgents killed; thousands of prisoners after the insurrection had been controlled; courts martial of alleged leaders; transportation without trial to overseas penal colonies; army patrols in the working-class areas making arbitrary searches, arrests, and confiscations'.[10] This was an example of a commissarial dictatorship, wielding police force but not legislative power. Nevertheless, this dictatorship of the sabre enabled the Assembly to pass counter-revolutionary measures such as the abolition of the ten-hour day and the closing down of the National Workshops, an institution that the working-class had won during the February revolution through its struggle against unemployment.[11]

The state of siege was maintained during the debate of the Constitution and officially ended on 19 October 1848. It has been argued that Cavaignac's dictatorship was the 'prelude to the modern history of the term'.[12] This dictatorship provided the basis for the state-of-siege provision that was introduced in the French Constitution of 4 November 1848, as Article 106. This in turn led to the law of 9 August 1849, which was still in force in the twentieth century as the fundamental law of 'constitutional dictatorship' in France.[13]

---

8 Draper, *The Dictatorship of the Proletariat*, 15.
9 Draper, *Karl Marx's Theory of Revolution*, 51.
10 Ibid.
11 Ibid., 52.
12 Draper, *The Dictatorship of the Proletariat*, 15.
13 Draper, *Karl Marx's Theory of Revolution*, 53.

Why was Cavaignac's dictatorship the prelude and not previous cases of similar institutions—such as the ones examined above—from 1789 to 1815? I believe the answer lies in the process of class struggle. From 1789 to 1815 (a period that covers the revolutionary uproar of the National Convention and the Committee of Public Safety, as well as Napoleon's regime) the bourgeoisie was still waging a battle of mainly progressive character against the feudal remnants of society, even though its reactionary arsenal against the new revolutionary elements was already developing. But by 1848 the bourgeois class had begun the process of consolidating its position as the ruling class. This required securing its rule against the new rising force of society (i.e. the proletariat), which was already recognised as the only force capable of fulfilling the modern goals of universal human emancipation.[14] The bourgeoisie had to adopt a counter-revolutionary viewpoint and develop institutions and ideological mechanisms that would allow it to reproduce its rule.[15]

This was the reason for the deployment of martial-law institutions in Paris, Berlin and Vienna later in 1848. Dictatorship spread throughout Europe. The crystallisation of the dominant class division for the centuries to come, between the ruling bourgeoisie and the rising proletariat, was the main reason for the development of the counter-revolutionary theory of dictatorship. The spectre of a Communist Revolution was translated into bourgeois ideology as a threat posed by a dictatorship of democracy, a dictatorship of the people. Here, the word dictatorship meant despotism or tyranny and echoed the fears expressed by Plato and Aristotle on the threats that a purely democratic regime posed to established society. It is interesting to note that, following the revolutionary upheavals of 1848, both the French—Francois Guizot, the last prime minister to serve under a French king—and the Prussian—Gottfried Ludolf Camphausen, a Rhenish capitalist—prime ministers identified the democratic movement and popular rule as a 'dictatorship of the people'.[16]

This dictatorship of the people had to be opposed by a dictatorship of the state. This argument was more characteristically developed by Juan Donoso Cortés, one of the Spanish counter-revolutionaries whose ideas greatly influenced the thought of Carl Schmitt. His 'Speech on Dictatorship' delivers many interesting points on a counter-revolutionary theory of dictatorship. There he begins by establishing

---

14 See Karl Marx, *Critique of Hegel's 'Philosophy of Right'* (Cambridge: Cambridge University Press, 2008).
15 See Herbert Macuse, *On Authority* (London: Verso, 2005).
16 Draper, *The Dictatorship of the Proletariat*, 16, 18.

that dictatorship is a form of government that is 'as legitimate, good, and beneficial a form as any other'.[17] The reason for this is found in the potential role of dictatorship in protecting the life of society. He compares society to a human body and says that both the human body and society may be invaded by forces, which in the case of the human body are called illnesses. In the case of society, when these invading forces are concentrated in political associations, 'the resisting forces concentrate themselves into the hands of one man'.[18] This is what he calls 'the clear, luminous, and indestructible theory of dictatorship'.[19]

It is obvious that, for Cortés, the invading forces are the political organisations of the proletariat that threaten the life of society. Cortés's celebration of the remedial function of dictatorship for the status quo clearly reflects the Roman principle of 'salus populi suprema lex esto': 'When the letter of the law is enough to save a society, then the letter of the law is best. But when it is not enough, then dictatorship is best'.[20] Saving society from 'illness' is the definition of 'salus populi'. Cortés's promotion of the institution of dictatorship ultimately rests on a distinction between two types of dictatorship: one that is beneficial for society (i.e. 'a dictatorship of Government') and one that is an illness for society (i.e. the 'dictatorship of insurrection'). He is able to capture both the democratic and the counter-revolutionary movements under the concept of dictatorship because, for him, dictatorial power is identified with omnipotence. We have already seen that he gives the example of the British Parliament as an institution that holds dictatorial power.[21] This point where dictatorship is identified with omnipotence (i.e. sovereign power) is of extreme importance for the further development of the theory of dictatorship and is echoed in Carl Schmitt's argument on dictatorship as the locus of sovereignty.

Cortés concludes his speech by openly advocating for a dictatorship of Government (i.e. a dictatorship from above) against a dictatorship from below, because the former comes from the most clean and serene regions. He chooses the 'dictatorship of the saber' and not the 'dictatorship of the dagger' because the former is more noble.[22] However, a commissarial type of dictatorship of the kind exercised under General Cavaignac did not prove sufficient to reproduce bourgeois rule in the aftermath of the 1848 revolutionary events in France. The socio-political

17 Cortés, *Speech on Dictatorship*, 46.
18 Ibid., 47.
19 Ibid.
20 Ibid., 46.
21 Ibid., 47.
22 Ibid., 59.

contradictions at play in that historical moment gave rise to the regime of Louis Bonaparte. Let us examine then what necessitated the change from Cavaignac to Bonaparte (i.e. from constitutional dictatorship to Bonapartism).

Bonapartism, Caesarism and dictatorship

In 1866, Friedrich Engels called Bonapartism 'the true religion of the modern bourgeoisie' in a letter to Karl Marx. He argued that the bourgeoisie does not possess the qualities required to rule directly itself and, therefore, a Bonapartist semi-dictatorship is its normal form of government.[23] What is meant by 'Bonapartist semi-dictatorship'? Why did Bonapartism assume such importance and capture the interest of several theorists, from Alexis de Tocqueville to Karl Marx, in the mid-nineteenth century? Can it be argued that a Bonapartist semi-dictatorship and not a republic is the proper form of bourgeois rule (i.e. the 'true religion' of the bourgeoisie)? These are some of the issues that this and the next couple of sections will deal with.

The term Bonapartism—as well as Caesarism—has been used to describe the regimes led by Napoleon Bonaparte and Louis Bonaparte in early and mid-nineteenth-century France, respectively. It has been suggested that the use of these concepts is associated with the following methodological questions on the approach to the two Bonaparte regimes: Did they consist of a novel form of rule or a form resembling that of Roman Caesaristic dictatorship?[24] Using the term Bonapartism arguably means approaching the two regimes as distinctively modern and French, rather than European or Western.[25] This approach would stress the similarities between the two regimes: their common basis on military coups that overthrew republican governments; their use of plebiscites based on universal suffrage; the founding of Empires that led military expeditions. On the other hand, using the term 'Caesarism' implies the acceptance of 'a pattern of significant recurrences under modern conditions of ancient political experiences dating back to the termination of the Roman Republic and the creation of the Principate'.[26] Such an approach would emphasise the elements common

---

23 Friedrich Engels, 'Engels to Marx, 13 April', in Karl Marx and Friedrich Engels, *Collected Works: Volume 42* (London: Lawrence and Wishart, 2010), 266.
24 Baher and Richter, *Dictatorship in History and Theory*, 11.
25 Melvin Richter, 'Tocqueville and French Nineteenth-Century Conceptualisations of the Two Bonapartes and Their Empires', in Baher and Richter, *Dictatorship in History and Theory*, 86.
26 Ibid., 86.

to Sulla's and Caesar's regimes, on the one hand, and Napoleon and Louis Bonaparte's, on the other: the rule by an individual; the seizure of power by force from elected representative governments; the establishment of an authoritarian, highly centralised and non-representative regime; a claim of plebiscitary legitimacy.

In his authoritative analysis of the regime of Louis Bonaparte, Karl Marx rejects the use of the term Caesarism at the outset. He argues that to use this concept is to unjustifiably ignore the differences between the material conditions of the ancient and the modern class struggles: 'in ancient Rome the class struggle took place only within a privileged minority, between the free rich and the free poor, while the great productive mass of the population, the slaves, formed the purely passive pedestal for these combatants'.[27] This is a point is of extreme importance because it emphasises that the function of juridico-political institutions is ultimately determined by class struggle and the level of socio-economic development.

The class struggle in Rome from the fifth to the first century BC, in France in the nineteenth century, or in Germany in the twentieth century, developed on different configurations of social forces. The use of the term dictatorship in all these contexts allows us to identify a common element: the adjustment of the state form to more authoritarian modes of exercise of class rule. But the fact that the term itself undergoes transmutations (several of which we have already discussed, namely, the change from constitutional to Caesaristic, or from commissarial to sovereign) points towards the impossibility of a single extra-historical meaning of the term and necessitates its examination always in the context of socio-political struggle. It is interesting to note with regards to Louis Bonaparte's regime that Marx does not opt for the term Bonapartism either, as he is aware of the differences in the configuration of class struggle between the two Bonapartist regimes too. Napoleon Bonaparte's regime was the result of the revolutionary struggle of the bourgeoisie to establish its rule in France and export its benefits to the rest of Europe. Louis Bonaparte's regime was the result of the counter-revolutionary struggle of the bourgeoisie against the new revolutionary social force, the proletariat.

The difference in character between Napoleon's and Louis's Bonapartist dictatorships is also captured in Antonio Gramsci's analysis. Gramsci was a prominent member of the Communist Party of Italy imprisoned by Mussolini's fascist dictatorship. Writing from prison, he used the term Caesarism to describe regimes as diverse as Caesar's,

---

27 Karl Marx, *The Eighteenth Brumaire of Louis Bonaparte*, 105.

Napoleon's, Louis Bonaparte's and Cromwell's, whose common element is that they all 'culminated in a great "heroic" personality'. According to Gramsci, 'Caesarism' expresses

> a situation in which the forces in conflict balance each other in a catastrophic manner; that is to say, they balance each other in such a way that a continuation of the conflict can only terminate in their reciprocal destruction.

In such cases a third force, C, may intervene from outside, subjugating what is left of both A and B.[28]

Gramsci tried to enrich this abstract schematic definition by distinguishing between progressive and reactionary forms of Caesarism, depending on the third force that provides the solution. When the intervening third force 'helps the progressive force to triumph', Caesarism is progressive. When it helps the reactionary force to triumph, it is reactionary. Caesar and Napoleon I are examples of the former, while Napoleon III and Bismarck signify the latter.[29] In addition, Gramsci distinguished between 'qualitative' and 'quantitative' Caesarism. The former, exemplified in Caesar and Napoleon, 'represented the historical phase of passage from one type of State to another type, in which the innovations were so numerous, and of such a nature, that they represented a complete revolution'. Contrariwise, in the case of Louis Bonaparte's 'quantitative' Caesarism, there was 'no passage from one type of State to another, but only "evolution" of the same type along unbroken lines'.[30]

There are certain problematic aspects in Gramsci's analysis. First, his theory of equilibrium seems abstract and extra-historical and cannot accurately explain the historical examples that have been characterised as Caesaristic or Bonapartist dictatorships. Gramsci's ambiguous terminology is also problematic in this respect. The analytical value of the term 'great heroic personality' is questionable, whereas the term 'type of state' used to distinguish between qualitative and quantitative Caesarism is not defined. Does the term 'type of state' signify the type of regime? Or does it refer to the issue of social revolution? If it signifies to the type of regime, then both Napoleon's and Louis Bonaparte's regimes should be called qualitative examples of Caesarism, as they both signified a

---

28 Antonio Gramsci, *Selections from the Prison Notebooks* (New York: International Publishers, 1992), 219.
29 Ibid.
30 Ibid., 222.

change from the republican to an imperial form. However, if it refers to the issue of social revolution, then why does Caesar's dictatorship fall within this scope?

The ambiguities and antinomies of Antonio Gramsci's work, which have enabled the subjection of the revolutionary aspects of his thought to reformist interpretations, are well documented.[31] Nevertheless, there are aspects of Gramsci's analysis of Caesarism that might be useful for our analysis of the different forms of dictatorship. Central among these is his association of Caesarist solutions with crises of authority or crises of hegemony. These appear in instances when the rule of the dominant class lacks widespread consensus and is unable to generate mechanisms of legitimation within society.[32] Gramsci saw the fascist dictatorship in Italy as resulting from the inability of the ruling class to move from an 'economic–corporate' to a 'hegemonic' phase of political development.[33] Caesarism, as a result of the breakdown of hegemony of the ruling class, is not necessarily this class's response to the rise of the dominated classes, but may be the result of intra-class contradictions (i.e. of the opposition of groups within the dominant bloc).

To grasp this point it is essential to briefly elaborate on Gramsci's view of the state and his concept of 'hegemony'. His general notion of state does not refer only to the set of institutions that exercise the monopoly of violence in society, but includes elements that need to be referred back to the notion of civil society. One of the definitions of the state provided by Gramsci is that of 'hegemony protected by the armour of coercion'.[34] It can be argued that in fulfilling its function of reproducing a regime of power, property and production relations, the state combines elements of repression and ideology, coercion and consent. In Marxist terms, coercion or repression refers to the mode of class rule enforced by violence, while ideology refers to the mode of class rule secured by consent. On this basis, the day-to-day reproduction of bourgeois rule and relations relies on the consent of the masses, in the form of the ideological belief that they exercise self-government through the state's representative institutions.[35] Simultaneously, violence plays a determinant role within the power structure of contemporary capitalism, as the system may resort to non-consensual measures in case of a crisis of hegemony or representation.[36]

---

31 See Perry Anderson, *The Antinomies of Antonio Gramsci* (London: Verso, 2017).
32 Fontana, *The Concept of Caesarism in Gramsci*, 183.
33 Ibid., 177.
34 Gramsci, *Selections from the Prison Notebooks*, 263.
35 Anderson, *The Antinomies of Antonio Gramsci*, 42.
36 Ibid.

Domination and leadership can thus be seen as two ways to exercise class rule based on predominantly repressive (domination) or ideological (leadership) means. However, emphasis must be put on the different class relations. The relation between antagonistic classes can only *appear* to be one of leadership. For instance, there can be no relation of true leadership between the capitalist class and the working class because their interests are essentially incompatible. Therefore, to the extent that the system of bourgeois rule can be reproduced on the basis of consensual means (e.g. through concessions affordable for the ruling class that serve its strategic interests of reproduction while also serving the immediate interests of the dominated classes), then the relationship between them can appear as one of leadership, and dictatorial solutions remain a latent possibility. On the contrary, a collapse of legitimacy in the political system might lead to a 'rush' to repression.

Dictatorship and crisis of hegemony

Let us now turn to examine the specific conditions that led to the establishment of the regime of Louis Bonaparte and assess the value of the above theoretical statements. We saw above that the February revolution led to the proletarian uprising of June and the crushing of the insurgency by Cavaignac's commissarial dictatorship. The bourgeois republic triumphed, with a variety of social forces on its side: the finance aristocracy, the industrial bourgeoisie, the middle class, the petty bourgeoisie, the army, the lumpenproletariat, the intellectuals, the clergy and the rural population. On the contrary, with 3,000 of the insurgents killed and 15,000 deported without trial, the proletariat receded into the background of the revolutionary stage.[37] This configuration of forces that eventually led to the Bonapartist dictatorship is far from an image of equilibrium, which Gramsci thought was an essential prerequisite of Caesarist solutions.

The bourgeois monarchy of Louis Philippe was thus followed by a bourgeois republic. Why a republic? It was, after all, the dictatorship of the sabre that saved society from its enemies. The answer lies in the advantages that the republican form offers for the consolidation and reproduction of class rule. As Marx showed in his 'Eighteenth Brumaire', and other Marxists in analyses of subsequent historical examples,[38] the republic is a state form that may mediate intra-class contradictions more

---

37 Karl Marx, *The Eighteenth Brumaire of Louis Bonaparte*, 110.
38 See Nicos Poulantzas, *The Crisis of Dictatorships: Portugal, Spain, Greece* (London: Verso, 1976).

effectively. According to Marx, the mass of the bourgeoisie in 1848 was divided into two sections: one section, the big landowners, had ruled during the Restoration with its priests and lackeys and was accordingly Legitimist; the other, the finance aristocracy and big industrialists, had ruled during the July monarchy with its lawyers, professors and smooth-tongued orators and was consequently Orleanist.[39]

These two factions were kept apart not so much by their principled loyalty to either of the royal houses, but by their 'material conditions of existence' (i.e. the 'two different kinds of property' on which their power rested: 'the old contrast between town and country, the rivalry between capital and landed property').[40] But the June insurrection had already united them in the Party of Order against the enemies of society. The republican form enabled the conjoint rule of these two class factions. The republican form, based on representation, deliberation in the legislative assembly and a multiplicity of political parties, would allow many diverse channels for the mediation of intra-class conflicts between these dominant class factions. This is why Marx describes the parliamentary republic as the unavoidable condition of the common rule of these class factions (i.e. 'the sole form of state in which their general class interest subjected to itself at the same time both the claims of their particular factions and all the remaining classes of society').[41] This point is of great value because the advantages that the republican form provides for the consolidation of bourgeois rule point towards the corresponding disadvantages of the dictatorial form.

Consequently, whereas 'a limited section of the bourgeoisie ruled in the name of the king, the whole of the bourgeoisie would now rule on behalf of the people'.[42] The main substantive change that the Constitution of 1848 brought was the institution of direct universal suffrage; otherwise, it was only a republicanised edition of the constitutional Charter of 1830.[43] The outcome of the sovereign dictatorship of the Constituent National Assembly, which carried out its work protected by Cavaignac's dictatorship of the sabre, was the constitutional enshrinement of the rights of liberty, freedom of the press, freedom of speech, of association, of assembly, of education and of religion.

---

39 Karl Marx, *The Eighteenth Brumaire of Louis Bonaparte*, 119–120.
40 Ibid., 128.
41 Ibid., 165.
42 Ibid., 110.
43 Ibid., 114.

As Marx notes, each of these freedoms was recognised as an inalienable right of the French citizens, but 'always with the marginal note that it is unlimited so far as it is not limited by the "equal rights of others and the public safety"'.[44] Thus, 'each paragraph of the Constitution contains its own antithesis, its own Upper and Lower House, namely, freedom in the general phrase, abrogation of freedom in the marginal note'.[45] This point reveals that the contradictions in the constitutional text are due to the operation of the principle of *salus populi*. The limitations to the enjoyment of these rights are always in the name of the public interest and in the interest of public safety or national security (i.e. in the interest of bourgeois safety).

The constitutional arrangement of 1848 would eventually influence the way that intra-class contradictions developed on the political plane, until Louis Bonaparte's coup in 1851. Marx locates the weakness of the constitution in its 'head'—or rather in 'the two heads in which it wound up—the Legislative Assembly, on the one hand, the President, on the other'. Articles 45 to 70 of the Constitution provided a constitutional procedure according to which the National Assembly could remove the President, but the President could only remove the National Assembly by setting aside the Constitution.[46] This had important consequences once the intra-class contradictions came to be expressed in the form of struggle between the two main institutions of government. On the one side there were 750 representatives of the people, elected by universal suffrage and eligible for re-election, who enjoyed legislative omnipotence. On the other side was the office of the President, held by a single individual, with authority to appoint and dismiss his ministers independently of the National Assembly, who could not serve consecutive terms (Article 45).

Perhaps the more interesting characteristic that separates these institutions is the type of representation that each of them secured. With regards to the National Assembly, the votes of the French citizens were split up among 750 members. Furthermore, each representative represents this or that party, this or that town or constituency. On the contrary, with regards to the President, all votes are concentrated on a single individual, who becomes 'the elect of the nation' and stands in a 'personal relation' to the nation.[47] This constitutional arrangement seems to foreshadow the one provided by the Weimar Constitution. In

44 Ibid.
45 Ibid., 115.
46 Ibid.
47 Ibid., 117.

fact, Marx's description of the relation between the two institutions is similar to Schmitt's politically motivated description of the Weimar Constitution. If we were to anachronistically use Schmittian terminology, we could describe the relationship between the people and the Assembly as one of 'representation', whereas the one between the people and the President was one of 'identity'.[48] The President seems like the institution that unites what is split in the election for the assembly. Thus, the President becomes the institution of choice for a system of rule in crisis.

Eventually the contradictions among the factions of the ruling class would play out in a conflict between the Assembly and the President, which led to the coup d'état of Louis Napoleon. The republican form was replaced by a Bonapartist dictatorship. I argue that the contradictory function of the republican form, with regards to the reproduction of bourgeois rule, to a great extent determines the contradictory disposition of the bourgeoisie towards the republic as a form of exercise of its rule. On the one hand, the republic enables the bourgeoisie to rule as a whole because it allows for the mediation of intra-class conflicts through its multiple channels of discussion and deliberation. On the other hand, the republican form may potentially undermine the rule of the bourgeoisie because the popular strata have access to the state mechanisms through the exercise of civil and political rights, through regular democratic elections, which *formally* permit the possibility of a working-class government (i.e. a government representing the interests of the majority class). This contradiction is well documented by Marx in his 'Class Struggles in France, 1848 to 1850'.

> The fundamental contradiction of this constitution, however, consists in the following: The classes whose social slavery the constitution is to perpetuate, proletariat, peasantry, petty bourgeoisie, it puts in possession of political power through universal suffrage. And from the class whose old social power it sanctions, the bourgeoisie, it withdraws the political guarantees of this power. It forces the political rule of the bourgeoisie into democratic conditions, which at every moment help the hostile classes to victory and jeopardise the very foundations of bourgeois society.[49]

---

48 See Carl Schmitt, *Constitutional Theory* (London: Duke University Press, 2008).
49 Karl Marx, 'Class Struggles in France, 1848 to 1850', in Karl Marx and Friedrich Engels, *Collected Works: Volume 10* (London: Lawrence and Wishart, 2010), 79.

How is this contradiction resolved? Or, rather, how is this contradictory relation between the bourgeoisie and the republican state form sustained? Marxist theory has approached this question on the basis of concepts such as ideology and hegemony. Historical experience has shown that bourgeois parliamentary elections would never produce a government dedicated to the expropriation of capital and the realisation of socialism. The reason for this arguably lies in the role of the state and ideology in the reproduction of bourgeois rule and capitalist relations of production. Bourgeois rule is not threatened by democratic elections because of the prior ideological conditioning of the proletariat before the electoral moment as such. Capitalist control of the means of communication (press, radio, television, new social media) based on the control of the means of production allows the bourgeoisie to promote its worldview and establish a great trust—through concessions, deception and fear—of the popular strata in the bourgeois representative institutions. From the initial conditioning by the family and the educational apparatus, to the constant conditioning by the media apparatus[50] propagating that 'there is no alternative', various and subtle ideological mechanisms operate on many levels in the capitalist social formation to ensure that the workers appear for work every day. Ideology ensures the hegemonic role of the bourgeoisie in a capitalist social formation and safeguards against the democratic threat.

But what happens when there is a crisis of hegemony? Ideology and rule by consent is only one of the modes of class rule. Ideology is always combined with repression and rule by coercion. If there is a crisis of representational institutions, to the extent that the bourgeoisie cannot mislead the popular strata by appearing as the 'leader' of society, then a state form predominantly based on coercion rather than consent might be necessary for the reproduction of bourgeois rule. In 1848 such a crisis of hegemony was even more acute because the bourgeois class was still in the process of consolidating its rule. It should not be forgotten that the republican bourgeois faction had attained power not through a liberal revolt of the bourgeoisie against the throne, but through the means of proletarian insurgency.[51] Despite the defeat of the proletariat in the June insurrection, the bourgeoisie still had to confront the subjugated classes and contend against them without mediation due to universal suffrage. By 1849 the main opposition party to the governing 'Party of Order' was the 'Montagne', the parliamentary name of the social-democratic

---

50 For a detailed analysis of the operation of ideological state apparatuses, see Louis Althusser, *On the Reproduction of Capitalism* (London: Verso, 2014).
51 Karl Marx, *The Eighteenth Brumaire of Louis Bonaparte*, 114.

party. In 1850 another revolutionary crisis threatened the bourgeois republic when Paris elected only Social-Democratic candidates in the by-elections of 10 March to fill the vacant seats of those representatives imprisoned or exiled following the June insurrection.

It was then that the bourgeoisie appreciated that bourgeois liberties threatened its rule and, therefore, had to abolish them by deeming them 'socialistic'. Having already turned from a revolutionary into a counter-revolutionary force of society, it realised that

> all the weapons it had forged against feudalism turned their points against itself, that all the means of education which it had produced rebelled against its own civilisation, . . . that all the so-called civil freedoms and organs of progress attacked and menaced its class rule at its social foundation and its political summit simultaneously'.[52]

As a result, a Damoclean sword had to hang over the bourgeoisie's head to safeguard its purse, and to restore tranquillity in the country, the bourgeois parliament had to be laid to rest.[53]

We come to the conclusion that the Bonapartist dictatorship was due to a crisis of hegemony of the bourgeois class, whose rule was threatened by the freedoms sanctioned in a republican state form. This crisis of hegemony was expressed in the form of a crisis of representative institutions. There was a crisis in the relation of the bourgeoisie to its spokesmen and scribes: representatives and represented were alienated from one another and no longer understood each other.[54] What is more, all the factions of the bourgeois class (finance capital, industrial capital and commercial capital) favoured Bonaparte as the 'guardian of Order' against the struggles of Parliament. They were all disturbed by and condemned the squabbles of the 'Party of Order' as a disturbance of order and demanded a return to normality and tranquillity.

The demand for a tranquil environment where capitalist production could develop and expand in conditions of normality played a major role in the establishment of the Bonapartist solution. This demand was augmented by the French crisis of overproduction in 1851, which the 'French bourgeoisie attributed to purely political causes, to the struggle between parliament and the executive power, to the precariousness of a merely provisional form of state' and to the terrifying prospect of the election for the next President in May 1852.[55] By November 1851, the

52 Ibid., 142.
53 Ibid., 143.
54 Ibid., 170.
55 Ibid., 174.

'Economist' had declared that 'the President is the guardian of order and is recognised as such on every Stock Exchange of Europe'.[56] However, the election for the President's office itself appeared as a destabilising factor. This was to become the default disposition of the bourgeoisie towards elections in times of crisis.

We can see then that the Bonapartist coup was a necessary result of developing contradictions.[57] The Bonapartist regime greatly enhanced the relative autonomy of the state from the ruling class. In 'forfeiting the Crown to save its purse' the bourgeoisie embraced its 'true religion'. This is the conclusion that Marx reached in analysing Louis Bonaparte's coup. All revolutions thus far had perfected the state machine instead of breaking it.[58] The first French Revolution developed what the absolute monarchy had begun (i.e. the centralisation of the state). This was perfected by Napoleon. In this stage, the state was 'only the means of preparing the class rule of the bourgeoisie'.[59] In the next stage of consolidation of bourgeois power, under the Restoration, under Louis Philippe and under the parliamentary republic, it was 'the instrument of the ruling class'.[60] The state machinery was perfected (i.e. it achieved maximum relative autonomy from the ruling class while representing its interests) under the second Bonaparte.

The state machine had consolidated its position so thoroughly that the 'Society of the 10th of December', a secret society of Bonapartist supporters comprised of opportunists and military leaders from the lumpenproletariat, could be considered as the ruling party of the Bonapartist regime. This does not mean that the lumpenproletariat became the ruling class simply because Bonaparte drew from its ranks the main supporters of his coup. Instead it indicates that the state's relative autonomy, an essential element for the exercise of class rule, was enhanced. This is what was meant by Engels when he called Bonapartism the 'true religion' of the bourgeoisie, namely, that a relatively autonomous state, whether republican or dictatorial, is essential for the reproduction of bourgeois rule.

This point has been further developed by Marxist theory to characterise the relation between the bourgeois class and the state as an objective relation. The state can be called capitalist by reason of the fact that it ensures the reproduction of bourgeois rule and the conditions of

56 Ibid., 170.
57 Ibid., 176.
58 Ibid., 186.
59 Ibid.
60 Ibid.

capital's profitability (i.e. the reproduction of capitalist relations of production). This relation is objective and does not require the direct participation of members of the ruling class in the state apparatus itself. In fact, despite the existence of close ties and interwoven networks between the ruling class and its representative, it could be argued that, especially in certain instances, the capitalist state might best serve the interests of the capitalist class only when the members of this class do not participate directly in the state apparatus.[61] This is a point we return to in the next chapter.

To conclude, this chapter focused on examining the types of dictatorship deployed in France during the process of consolidation of bourgeois rule. Cavaignac's dictatorship and the Bonapartist dictatorship could be seen, respectively, as examples of a constitutional dictatorship and a dictatorial regime in the modern sense of the term. More importantly, we established that taking into account the specific balance of social forces and the process of class struggle is essential if one is to analyse the developments in the state form and the accompanying developments in state theory, as well as political jargon. In this context the modern sense of dictatorship was developed to signify an adjustment of the state form towards authoritarianism, relying predominantly on coercion, following a crisis of hegemony.

---

61 Nicos Poulantzas, 'The Problem of the Capitalist State', in *The Poulantzas Reader: Marxism, Law and the State* (London: Verso, 2008), 179.

3 Dictatorship and reproduction of bourgeois power

By the early twentieth century, capitalism had entered its highest stage (i.e. the imperialist stage). According to the theory of imperialism, the highest stage of capitalism is characterised by the transition from free competition to monopoly production and the formation of monopolist trusts, cartels and banks. The merging of bank capital and industrial capital leads to the creation of a financial oligarchy. This is a result of the law of capitalist accumulation and the tendency of capitalist firms to seek increasingly greater profits. In addition, export and direct investment of capital in countries with underdeveloped economies, as a means to generate greater profits, replaces the export of commodities. A direct consequence of this is that international monopolist businesses, and the great powers that support them, divide the world among themselves.[1]

A phenomenon central to the imperialist stage is the increasingly important role of the state in ensuring the conditions for capital's profitability. This refers not only to the requirement of a strong army that protects the colonial and international expansion of monopoly capital, or with the involvement of national armies in imperialist wars. It also refers to the state's role in regulating the capitalist relations of production, for instance, through labour legislation. Labour law poses a relative limit to capital's thirst for profit so as not to exhaust labour power. Furthermore, it regulates competition between monopolies, and functions as a pressure valve for workers' indignation. The state apparatus grows ever stronger in ensuring the reproduction of conditions of exploitation by suppressing and deflating the working-class movement. One phenomenon related to this process is that of labour aristocracy, whereby the creation of a compromised upper stratum of the working class takes a leading position to promote a policy of class compromise,

---

1 V.I. Lenin, 'Imperialism: The Highest Stage of Capitalism', in *Collected Works: Volume 22* (Moscow: Progress Publishers, 1974), 265.

48 *Reproduction of bourgeois power*

enabled by the super-profits yielded by the colonial expansion and exploitation.

In the aftermath of the imperialist war of 1914–1918, another development shook the dominant capitalist states and threatened the reproduction of the leading position of their ruling classes: the October Revolution of 1917. The establishment of a first workers' state, a new form of state organisation based on the institution of workers' councils, led to a pan-European movement, a revolutionary wave that threatened the foundation of world capitalism. To this revolutionary wave the bourgeois state responded in different ways, with different mixtures of the elements of repression and concessions. In the interwar period, following a brief process of stabilisation, the capitalist crisis of 1929 created conditions favourable for yet another working-class revolt. In many capitalist states the new crisis was dealt with through the establishment of dictatorial regimes. This chapter, for reasons of brevity and clarity of the argument, focuses on one of them and analyses the case of the Nazi dictatorship, established in 1933 in Germany, and the various concepts that have been used to approach this regime, such as dictatorship, totalitarianism, Caesarism and fascism.

Of course there is an abundance of historical examples that could be used to illustrate the role that the concept and institution of dictatorship have played in the process of reproducing capitalism, such as Italian fascism, Franco's regime, the Metaxas dictatorship as well as the Colonels' dictatorship in Greece, or the various right-wing military dictatorships that had been installed or at least supported by the United States in Latin American countries. However, I have chosen to examine one paradigmatic historical example in much more depth, rather than proceed with a superficial comparative overview of several historical cases.

Nazi dictatorship

Let me begin the analysis with Giorgio Agamben's claim that the Nazi state was in reality a state of emergency that was never revoked.[2] According to Agamben, since the 'Decree for the Protection of the People and the State of 28 February 1933 was never repealed, the entire Third Reich can be considered a state of exception that lasted twelve years'.[3] I will argue instead that a careful reading of Schmitt's

---

2 Giorgio Agamben, *From the State of Law to the Security State*, available at Autonomies, 28 December 2015, http://autonomies.org/pt/2015/12/from-the-state-of-law-to-the-security-state-giorgio-agamben-on-the-state-of-emergency-in-france/.
3 Agamben, *State of Exception*, 2.

Dictatorship, together with his *State, Movement, People*, prohibits such conclusion being reached.

Can the Nazi state be accurately described as a permanent state of exception? Are the Schmittian terms, sovereign and commissarial dictatorship, useful for answering this question? To answer this, we have to look at Schmitt's celebratory essay on the Nazi state, his 1933 *State, Movement, People*. There, Schmitt refutes the argument that

> the National-Socialist public law has only the value of a temporary, interim measure against the background of the earlier constitution, and that a simple bill passed by the Reichstag might again abolish the new constitutional legislation entirely and return to the Weimar Constitution'.[4]

He argues instead that there are two issues to be considered with regards to the Enabling Act (i.e. the act amending the Weimar Constitution that gave the German executive the power to enact laws without the involvement of the Reichstag parliament) of 24 March 1933. First, the elections of March 1933 'were in fact *a popular referendum, a plebiscite*, by which the German people has acknowledged Adolf Hitler, the leader of the National-Socialist Movement, as the political leader of the German people'.[5] According to Schmitt, the people appears here and gives ordinary elections the character of a plebiscite. The *pouvoir constituant* and the *will of the people* are invoked by Schmitt as foundational for the Nazi state. This invocation points towards the concept of sovereign dictatorship with regards to the emergence of the Nazi state. Second, Schmitt emphasises the importance of the fact that this transition should take place legally.[6] The Enabling Act came into legal existence in conformity with Article 76 of the Weimar Constitution, which required a two-thirds majority for laws amending the Constitution. But that 'does not mean that one may still nowadays consider the Weimar Constitution as the foundation of the present-day State structure, but only that the law represents a bridge from the old to the new State, from the old base to the new base'.[7]

One could argue that the two aforementioned legal instruments, the 'Decree for the Protection of the People and the State' of 28 February 1933 (known as the 'Reichstag Fire Decree'), passed under

---

4 Schmitt, *State, Movement, People*, 5.
5 Ibid. (emphasis in original).
6 Ibid., 6.
7 Ibid.

the emergency provision of Article 48 of the Weimar Constitution, and the 'Enabling Act' of 24 March 1933, correspond to the different types of dictatorship—the former being an instance of commissarial while the latter is an instance of sovereign dictatorship. Both, however, facilitated the consolidation of Nazi rule, in intricate relation with the notion of the people; the former protecting the people, the latter being an expression of the people's constituent power. Commissarial dictatorship and sovereign dictatorship show their indissolvability at this point, as they are both necessary to deal with the internal enemy. Yet the latter involves the overthrow of the previous regime and the establishment of a new more efficient one, through the exercise of law-making powers, to deal with this enemy.

According to Schmitt, this element of *efficiency* refers to the ability to make the political decision on who is the friend and who the enemy. Based on the above, it is argued that *State, Movement, People* is the key to understanding Schmitt's theory of sovereignty and the exception. Until then, Schmitt had not named who the enemy was. His theory had already taken sides, but the enemy remained unnamed. The Nazi state form is different from the Weimar Republic in terms of its efficiency in dealing with the internal enemy (i.e. the organised working-class movement and the Communist Party) and, thus, ensuring the reproduction of capitalist social relations in the face of rising contradictions.[8]

In *State, Movement, People* it becomes clear that the political premium[9] should not be exploited by the Communists, but it has to be exploited by the Nazi Party to safeguard the bourgeois State with the passing of the Enabling Act. This provides us with the substantive content of Carl Schmitt's decisionistic theory. The new form of the Nazi state can make the political decision and crush the enemy who threatens the reproduction of bourgeois rule; and this is what the old form of the Rechtstaat could not deal with efficiently.

The change in the state form was accompanied by a conceptual shift in the main legitimating mechanism. Therefore, the notion of political unity, which in Schmitt's 1928 work, *Constitutional Theory*, serves as the basis of the constitution-making power of a unified people, gives its place to the principles of 'leadership' (Führerprinzip)[10] and 'ethnic

---

8 One could not wait for the empowerment of a system that, by its own weakness and neutrality, was in no way capable of recognising even a mortal enemy of the German people, in order to abolish the Communist Party, the enemy of the State and of the people. Schmitt, *State, Movement, People*, 3.
9 Carl Schmitt, *Legality and Legitimacy* (London: Duke University Press, 2004).
10 'The primary importance of the political leadership is a fundamental principle of the present-day public law'. Schmitt, *State, Movement, People*, 8–9.

identity', which can accommodate more efficiently the most aggressive form of reactionary policies of the capitalist state. This new notion of the people, identified with the Führer, is the new foundational and legitimating principle of the Nazi state. However, the ideological function served by both notions is the same: the construction of an abstract people, of a unified whole that obscures the fundamental division between exploiting and exploited classes.

This marks the passage from a 'quantitative total state' (a welfare state with a pluralist party system representing different class interests) to a 'qualitative total state' (a strong one-party state to represent the interests of the ruling class), to use Schmitt's definition. Elections in the former, as was the case under the Weimar Constitution, had become an option that split the German people into many incompatible parties. On the contrary, elections in the qualitative total state, such as the German elections of 12 November 1933, were part of 'the great plebiscite on which the German people assume a foremost position in the politics of the Reich government by responding to the appeal launched by the political leadership'.[11] According to Schmitt, the one-party Nazi state is the form corresponding to the truly unified people now substantively unified on the basis of ethnic identity and the Führerprinzip. This form promotes the ideology of class collaboration, which accompanied the new level of intensified exploitation. Moreover, it ensures the consolidation of bourgeois rule through the amelioration of intra-class conflicts and the elimination of centrifugal tendencies.

The Nazi state form combined repressive (e.g. the ability to identify the 'internal enemy' and violently suppress the working-class movement) with ideological elements (promoting the principle of class collaboration through the notion of 'political unity'). In this context of intensified contradictions that threatened the reproduction of capitalism, Schmitt provides a political theory of authoritarian capitalism in which authoritarian political institutions are masked by an appearance of popular legitimacy.[12] Schmitt's proposal for a qualitative total state empowers capital by freeing it from the regulatory burdens of the democratic welfare state, while his plebiscitarianism drastically curtails genuine popular participation. This type of state provides for the 'legal and institutional preconditions for a system in which capitalist proprietors engage in conscious forms of joint supervision of the economy'.[13]

11 Ibid., 10–11.
12 Scheuerman, *Carl Schmitt: The End of Law*, 101.
13 Ibid., 103–104.

Schmitt's advocating for a qualitative total state that guarantees authentic state sovereignty while simultaneously managing to provide substantial autonomy to owners of private capital, appears in his 1933 essay, 'A Strong State and Sound Economics',[14] based on a speech he presented to a prominent organisation of German industrialists, the Langnamverein, when he called for a 'rollback of the state [economy] to a natural and correct amount'.[15] The 'qualitative total state' must replace its 'quantitative' counterpart, a weak, social-democratic-inspired interventionist state. The capitalist economy should be 'self-administered', meaning that the 'economic leaders', owners and managers need to be given substantial autonomy in their industries and factories, and they need to be freed from social-democratic forms of regulation.[16]

Schmitt's argument here is still one of efficiency, not only in terms of making the political decision on the friend and enemy, but also with regards to economic planning: for Schmitt, the economically dominant should plan and the state should provide the legal and institutional preconditions. Therefore, the dictatorial form safeguards the bourgeois rule not only in eradicating the communist threat but also in promoting and consolidating the interests of monopoly capital. Indeed, in both its program and its fact, the Nazi dictatorship safeguarded the fundamental condition for the reproduction of capitalist relations (i.e. private property). In his first Reichstag speech on 25 March 1933, Adolf Hitler said: 'The government will on principle safeguard the interests of the German Nation not by roundabout ways of bureaucracy organised by the state but by encouraging private initiative and by recognising private property'.[17]

14 See Schmitt, 'Starker Staat und gesunde Wirtschaft: Ein Vortrag vor Wirtschaftsführern', in 2(1933) *Volk und Reich*, 89–90; Schmitt, 'Machtpositionen des modernen Staates' (1933), in Schmitt, *Verfassungsrechtliche Aufsätze aus den Jahren 1924–1954* (Berlin: Duncker & Humblot, 1958), 371. A translation is found in Cristi, *Carl Schmitt and Authoritarian Liberalism*, 212.
15 Scheuerman, *Carl Schmitt: The End of Law*.
16 An example of this self-administration of capital, enabled by the qualitative total state, can be found in an order of the Minister of Economics of 12 November 1936, which transferred a great deal of responsibility for the supervision of the activities of the cartels from governmental authorities to bodies of the economic self-administration. The Minister wrote: 'It is my intention to obtain the co-operation of private economic organisations in the execution of the supervisory activities of the cartels which my ministry has hitherto exercised alone. The administrative bodies of the private economic organisations should be responsible for seeing that the cartels are in harmony with the economic policy of the government in every respect'; see Ernst Fraenkel, *The Dual State: A Contribution to the Theory of Dictatorship* (New York: The Lawbook Exchange, Ltd., 2010), 97.
17 Fraenkel, *The Dual State*, 60.

Nazism as totalitarianism

Schmitt's distinction between a quantitative and a qualitative total state may be considered as a manifestation of—or at least as influenced by—the tradition of authoritarian liberalism that emerged towards the end of the Weimar Republic, as a new mode of ordoliberal response to the then crisis of capitalism. A noted neoliberal economist, Alexander Rüstow, did not hesitate to confirm the 'liberal ancestry' of Schmitt's conception of the 'total state'.[18] In distinction to laissez-faire liberalism, authoritarian liberalism assigned the task of ensuring the constitution of economic freedom to the state. From this standpoint the premise of free economy is the 'strong state'.[19] The 'weak state' is dismissed because it is unable to defend itself against the demands of the popular classes. It does not set limits to contesting social forces and fails to depoliticise the socio-economic relations on the basis of a rule-based system of market interaction..[20] Only the strong state can distinguish itself from society and prevent government from becoming 'prey' to powerful private interests and class-specific demands.[21]

An essential prerequisite for the protection of 'private capitalist enterprise' by the strong state is the deep politicisation of all private matters, as every issue can be deemed a political issue and therefore an issue that draws on the friend–enemy question, according to Schmitt. This is accompanied by an equally radical process of de-politicisation, as a strong state can only be a state that has dealt and done away with the multiple organisations (political parties, trade unions, etc.) that seek to express the views of their social members and contest for state power. By the early 1920s another term of a common origin was coined in Italy to describe such desires of the ruling classes—'totalitarianism'. In fact, it has been argued that Schmitt's theory of the qualitative total state was greatly influenced by similar formulations of Vilfredo Pareto, who espoused political authoritarianism and economic liberalism simultaneously and influenced the early economic policies of Mussolini.[22] By 1925, Mussolini had usurped the term 'totalitarian', speaking of the 'fierce totalitarian will' of his Movement. Giovanni Gentile, the chief

---

18 Scheuerman, *Carl Schmitt: The End of Law*, 31.
19 Werner Bonefeld, 'European Economic Constitution and the Transformation of Democracy: On Class and the State of Law', 21 *European Journal of International Relations*, 867, 869.
20 Ibid., 873.
21 Ibid., 874.
22 Franz L. Neumann, *Behemoth: The Structure and Practice of National Socialism, 1933–1944* (Chicago: Ivan R. Dee Publisher, 2009), 49.

ideologue of Italian fascism, also employed the term on numerous occasions, though in a more étatist sense similar to Schmitt's, implying an all-embracing state that would overcome the state–society divide of weak pluralist democracies.[23]

However, the term 'totalitarianism', originating in the interwar period and sharing common origins with the current of authoritarian liberalism and Schmitt's theory of the qualitative total state, soon acquired a life of its own and transcended its meaning as a signifier of the desires of the European ruling classes in crisis. It is well established, although still not common knowledge, that this development was politically motivated and served a vital role in the ideological class struggle between the bourgeois and the proletarian worldviews. Already in the 1920s the term was used by bourgeois writers to associate both 'right-wing' and 'left-wing' parties as the 'totalitarian enemies' of democracy, to counter the Marxist analyses of Nazism as a form of fascism engendered by capitalism in crisis.[24] The first usage of the word 'totalitarianism' to bracket together fascist and communist states seems to have been in England in 1929. It kept gaining ground in the Anglo-Saxon countries during the 1930s, in the context of intensified contradictions for the main European powers that felt threatened by German expansionism but even more threatened by the rise of the working-class movement that contested their rule from within.[25]

During the Cold War era, totalitarianism theories (developed by German expatriates in the U.S., like Hannah Arendt and Carl Friedrich, as well as thinkers in Western European countries, such as Karl Dietrich Bracher and Raymond Aron) dominated the academic discourse and had far-reaching influence on many political and legal documents, as well as the common-sense understanding of politics. Eventually these theories crumbled under the weight of detailed accumulated research, only to re-emerge after the fall of the Soviet regimes. Thereafter, they played a central role in a renewed process of historical revisionism whose goal was to delegitimize the revolutionary tradition to reiterate the argument that the history of modern democracy is exclusively identified with the history of liberalism, which triumphed at the end of the Cold War.[26]

---

23 Ian Kershaw, *The Nazi Dictatorship* (London: Bloomsbury Academic, 2015), 26.
24 Ibid., 23.
25 Ibid., 27.
26 Stefano G. Azzarà, 'A Left-Wing Historical Revisionism: Studying the Conflicts of the Twentieth Century After the Crisis of Anti-Fascist Paradigm', 3 *Crisis and Critique*, 411.

Reproduction of bourgeois power 55

These theories equate Nazism and communism, while paying no attention to the differences in class rule, relations of production, political goals and ideological foundation between the Nazi and the Soviet regime. They assess the Ribentrop–Molotov agreement as a mere sign of confirmation of the shared characteristics between these regimes, while erasing the earlier isolation of the Soviet regime from the Western world, the intervention of fourteen capitalist states in 1918 in aid of the counterrevolution, as well as the anti-fascist paradigm born during the Second World War from the alliance between the liberal democracies and the Soviet Union.[27] Nevertheless, despite the analyses of numerous—and not just Marxist, but also bourgeois—thinkers and especially historians that discredit totalitarian theories, the term 'totalitarianism' is still universally accepted as a scientific category, even by those who continue to call themselves Marxists, or are close to Marxism. For example, it goes without saying that any attempt to reassess the question of Stalin's role in the twentieth century would lead to a collision course with a common feeling that is still deeply rooted both in the academic community and, more generally, in the global political culture.[28] The far-reaching influence of these theories in the scientific, political and common-sense understanding of the state is evident in a variety of official documents, such as the European Parliament resolution of 2 April 2009 on European conscience and totalitarianism,[29] or the European Commission Statement of 23 August 2017 on the Europe-Wide Day of Remembrance for the victims of all totalitarian and authoritarian regimes,[30] as well as the Declaration of the European Parliament that proclaimed 23 August as European Day of Remembrance for Victims of Stalinism and Nazism.[31]

One of the major exponents of the theory of totalitarianism was Hannah Arendt, whose work, *The Origins of Totalitarianism*,[32] has been one of the most widely disseminated and highly influential works on the subject. In it, Arendt fully assimilates the socialist (Soviet) and Nazi

27 Ibid.
28 Ibid., 413.
29 European Parliament, *Resolution of 2 April 2009 on European Conscience and Totalitarianism* (P6_TA(2009)0213).
30 European Commission, *Statement by First Vice-President Timmermans and Commissioner Jourová on the Europe-Wide Day of Remembrance for the Victims of All Totalitarian and Authoritarian Regimes* (STATEMENT/17/2722).
31 European Parliament, *Declaration of the European Parliament on the Proclamation of 23 August as European Day of Remembrance for Victims of Stalinism and Nazism* (P6_TA(2008)0439).
32 Hannah Arendt, *The Origins of Totalitarianism* (New York: Harcourt, Inc., 1976).

state form under a new category of state, the totalitarian state. Arendt's definition of the totalitarian system identifies as its central characteristic the intentional and consciously organised effort for the elimination of the intermediate relations between individuals (private, personal, family, professional, social, class, etc.), and their absorption by the state and its unique ideology, in such a way that each separate, important or insignificant issue is transformed into an ideologico-political issue that touches the core of the state. This dialectics of politicisation and de-politicisation ultimately leads to the transformation of the people-citizens into an undifferentiated mass of subjects without other political characteristics outside those of the state servant.

Arendt's description of the main characteristic of the totalitarian system is astonishing in its similarities with the mainstream description of bourgeois democracy and the people as its main condition for legitimation. In his *Constitutional Theory*, Schmitt describes the bourgeois model of democracy, which is based on a formal conception of the people. The people appear in order to dress the decisions made by the political representatives of the ruling class in the garments of sovereignty. But this people is a formal, abstract people devoid of social content. Political parties of the exploited classes, social groups and trade unions must have no political voice of their own. They must not be allowed to express their own economic and political interests. Schmitt considers the people to be 'present' as a political entity only when engaged in *acclamation* and 'to the extent that it does not only appear as an organised interest group'.[33]

Schmitt's model of democracy can hardly be characterised as marginal. Despite its compatibility with authoritarianism, it has to be noted that it shares common origins with the mainstream conception of bourgeois democracy. Let us take Jean-Jacques Rousseau's theory of the general will, for example. Contrary to earlier, pre-modern conceptions of the state, which presented it as the expression of divine will or openly as the will of the ruling class, the bourgeois conception of the state presents it as an expression of the general will of the nation. However, Rousseau claims that the general will can only be expressed if the private interests and the excesses and insufficiencies associated with these are eliminated. On the contrary, 'when there are intrigues, and partial associations arise at the expense of the greater one, the will of each of these associations becomes general in relation to its members and particular in relation to the state'.[34] Rousseau concludes that if the general

33 Carl Schmitt, *Constitutional Theory*, 272.
34 Jean-Jacques Rousseau, *The Social Contract*, 66.

will is to be properly ascertained, 'there should be no partial society within the state' and 'each citizen should decide according to his own opinion'.[35]

Thus, even for one of the theoretical sources of the mainstream conception of liberal democracy, the people should appear merely as a sum of individuals—similar to the Thatcherite axiom by which only individuals exist in society, not social classes with distinct social interests. This condition of legitimation of state power is essentially a fiction designed and reproduced so as to sustain a false consciousness on behalf of the dominated classes. The highest political organisation of society (i.e. the state) is presented as the political organisation of the 'whole people'— therefore, of all classes—when it is only a set of institutions that consolidate and reproduce the rule of the dominant class. The bourgeois state has to silence all particular class organisations to express the 'general will' of the nation. This bourgeois state relies on a formal conception of the people, *devoid of any social class content*, which serves as its legitimating basis.

Consequently, the absence (or elimination) of class organizations of the dominated classes, defined by the theorists of totalitarianism as one of its root causes, is a permanent trait of the bourgeois state (i.e. a precondition of its legitimacy). The question then arises: if the main characteristic of totalitarian regimes is an essential precondition of the liberal-democratic state, does this mean that everything is totalitarianism?

This is only one of the substantial criticisms raised not only by theorists who categorically reject this concept as having no analytical value, but also by those who do not reject it out of hand, but see its application as very limited. For example, it has been argued that the concept of totalitarianism can only generally and superficially describe the similarities of systems that, on closer inspection, are very different. It says very little to refer to both Nazi Germany and Soviet Russia as 'one-party states' given the entirely different structures and functions of the state institutions of these different regimes (the latter originally erected on a system of workers' councils, while the former was dominated by the political police).[36] Equally misleading are the generalisations emanating from this concept with regards to the nature of the Nazi and the Soviet economic systems, the former being an aggressive imperialist economy seeking expansion and new areas of profitability while the latter was an

---

35 Ibid., 67.
36 Kershaw, *The Nazi Dictatorship*, 42.

economy in the process of establishing socialisation of the means of production and a direction towards satisfying social needs.

Furthermore, it has been argued that perhaps the decisive disadvantage of totalitarianism as an analytical concept is that it says nothing about the socio-economic conditions, functions and political aims of a system, but is 'content to rely solely upon emphasis of techniques and overt forms of rule'.[37] This is evident in the mainstream definition of totalitarianism, which popularised the term during the Cold War and established it as the blueprint for any research conducted on the Soviet or fascist political forms. In their *Totalitarian Dictatorship and Autocracy*, Carl Friedrich and Zbigniew Brzezinski identified six defining characteristics of the 'totalitarian system': an elaborate guiding ideology; a single mass party led by a dictator; a system of terror, using a set of repressive measures such as a secret police; a monopoly on the control of weapons; a monopoly on the control of means of communication; and a central direction and control of the economy through state planning.[38] These traits focus exclusively on systems and techniques of rule and pay no attention whatsoever to the differences in the social, productive, distributive or property relations, or to the socio-economic processes that necessitated the fascist dictatorships. Issues discussed in the next sections, such as the social composition of fascist parties and the relationship of fascist movements to the existing ruling class, are of little importance to the totalitarianism theorist.[39]

Nazism as Caesarism

The issue of the class character of the Nazi state form is crucial to grasp the relationship between the dictatorial form and the law. It is essential to understand that the Nazi state was not a state of pure arbitrariness and permanent state of exception; rather, it represented a new normality that reproduced elements of the old legal order that were essential for the functioning of a capitalist economy. This chapter discusses one of the most significant theoretical approaches to the question of the class character of the Nazi state, namely, Poulantzas's analysis of fascist dictatorships. In his *Fascism and Dictatorship*, Poulantzas deals with the two fascist states of the Axis powers (i.e. fascist Italy and Nazi

---

37 Ibid., 43.
38 Carl Joachim Friedrich and Zbigniew K. Brzezinski, *Totalitarian Dictatorship and Autocracy* (Boston: Harvard University Press, 1965).
39 Kershaw, *The Nazi Dictatorship*, 176.

Germany) in parallel. This chapter discusses the aspects of his analysis on the Nazi state.

Poulantzas's analysis of dictatorship emphasises the level of development of capitalist relations, as well as the specificity of class struggle. These factors ultimately determine the specific form that the exceptional state assumes to respond to the crisis. This form is usually shaped by a major displacement of the dominant branch of the state apparatus. As we saw in the previous chapter, a crisis of hegemony (i.e. a crisis in the ruling class's capacity to reproduce its position predominantly on consensual means) may result in an alteration in the mode of exercise of public power and a heavier reliance on force rather than on consent. The specific apparatus that holds the dominant position specifies the form of the regime of the exceptional state. Thus, according to Poulantzas, the army is dominant in a military dictatorship; the civil administration in Bonapartism; and the political police in the fascist state.[40]

Indeed, the development of the political police apparatus within a few years following the Nazi party's rise to power is evidence of its dominant role in the restructured state apparatus: the unification of all local police forces in 1933, followed by the fusion of the political police (Gestapo) and the SS under a single command in 1934 and by the ultimate fusion of all the police forces under the dominance of SS-Gestapo in 1936.[41] The role of this state branch was both repressive and ideological. Extensive powers were conferred on this apparatus, and its sphere and scope of intervention became unlimited, including the army, the administration, the judiciary and the Nazi party, and concerning not only 'security matters, but also administrative and military questions'.[42] The constitutional source for this kind of authority was the principle of leadership. The political police was seen as the direct incarnation of the will of the leader and this principle legitimised this branch as the central element of the Nazi regime's exceptionality. The role of this branch of the state and its source of legitimacy also resulted in major modifications in the juridical system—a point we shall return to later.

Despite the fruitful elements of Poulantzas's analysis of the fascist dictatorship as a type and form of state, his whole argument on the class nature of this state proceeds from a rather contradictory premise. To begin with, Poulantzas rejects Gramsci's Caesarism and Thalheimer's Bonapartism, but his analysis is more Gramscian than he cares to

---

40 Nicos Poulantzas, *Fascism and Dictatorship: The Third International and the Problem of Fascism* (London: Verso, 2019), 318.
41 Ibid., 341.
42 Ibid., 342.

admit. We briefly outlined the main elements of Gramsci's Caesarism in the previous chapter. Similarly, August Thalheimer examined the Nazi dictatorship as a case of Bonapartism. Thalheimer located the essential factor of the political crisis that gives rise to Bonapartism as an equilibrium between the two main class forces, the bourgeoisie and the proletariat.[43] In such a situation the former has to sacrifice its 'political domination' for the benefits of a 'Bonapartist' figure, a 'saviour' third force, to preserve its 'socio-economic dominance'.[44] This process contributes to the enhanced relative autonomy of the Bonapartist state from the dominant classes. This is all quite similar to Gramsci's analysis of 'Caesarism' as the result of a particular equilibrium.

Yet, we saw in the previous chapter that there is no 'equilibrium' in Marx's analysis of Bonapartism in the 'Eighteenth Brumaire'. The revolutionary proletariat was already defeated in June 1848 and remained in the background of the social struggles that led to the Bonapartist coup. The main reason that necessitated the Bonapartist dictatorship had to do with the difficulties of the bourgeoisie to reproduce its rule. Its position as a hegemonic class was not yet consolidated and the weapons it had forged to rise to power against the feudal class had then turned their points against it. So it needed to 'give up the sword' to 'save its purse'. Initially Poulantzas seems to be making a similar point with regards to fascist dictatorship. He held that the working class had already been thoroughly defeated by the time fascism came to power.[45] This view has an element of truth in it, insofar as it leads to the examination of intra-class contradictions and the role they played in the establishment of the Nazi state form. However, if the working class was thoroughly defeated, why the need to crush its organisations? Resort to repression would have been redundant unless the interests of the dominant class were threatened by the continued existence of the class organisations of the dominated classes.

Poulantzas's view was that the fascist dictatorship arose from the failure of the two principle classes of capitalist society (i.e. the bourgeoisie and the proletariat) to establish hegemony over German society. This failure enabled the petty bourgeoisie to act as the 'third force' through its political organisation—the Nazi party. According to Poulantzas, the petty bourgeoisie, through the fascist party, becomes the 'ruling class' during the first period of fascism, as well as the 'class

---

43 August Thalheimer, *On Fascism*, 1930, available at www.marxists.org/archive/thalheimer/works/fascism.htm.
44 Poulantzas, *Fascism and Dictatorship*, 60.
45 Dylan Riley, 'Foreword', in Poulantzas, *Fascism and Dictatorship*, xiii.

in charge of the State', without ever becoming the 'politically dominant class'.[46]

Thus, Poulantzas seems to be introducing a distinction between the politically dominant class and the ruling class (and possibly even the class in charge of the state). This is arguably a problematic conceptualisation of the relationship between the state and social classes because it seems to identify the ruling class with the class in charge of the state, rather than with the politically dominant class. In Poulantzas's theoretical schema the petty bourgeoisie is the ruling class because its political organisation (i.e. the fascist party) is the party in charge of the state, whereas the politically dominant class—the bourgeoisie—is not in charge of the state, at least in the first period of fascism. Of course, this view leads to questions regarding the issue of class rule and class nature of the state. Does this mean that in the first period of fascism we can speak of a state of the petty bourgeoisie? Does the existence of intra-class contradictions or the inability to 'lead' lead to a loss of class rule/state power?

I argue that Poulantzas's terminology is rather problematic at this point and seems to adopt the Gramscian view of the equilibrium that he started by rejecting. A crisis of hegemony by no means entails that the bourgeoisie loses its ruling position in the capitalist social formation. What is compromised is the bourgeoisie's ability to reproduce its rule and domination predominantly on the basis of ideological means, hence the need for the conduit of a political organisation of petty bourgeois origins. This becomes clear if we imagine a different scenario: if the political personnel of the governing party are recruited by the working class, does this make it the ruling class? For instance, in the case of the coalition governments of the Social Democratic Party (SPD) in Germany, did the working class become the ruling class?

Furthermore, Poulantzas's distinction between the politically dominant class and the ruling class seems to contradict his own analysis of the state. As we saw above, for Poulantzas, the relation between the bourgeois class and the state is an objective relation.[47] In fact, he argued that while members of the state apparatus belong, by their class origin, to different classes, their class origin and class situation recedes into the background in relation to their class position. This means that they belong precisely to the state apparatus and that they have as their objective function the actualisation of the role of the state.[48] This view

---

46 Poulantzas, *Fascism and Dictatorship*, 87.
47 Poulantzas, *The Poulantzas Reader*, 178.
48 Ibid., 179.

seems to contradict the idea that the class in charge of the state is also the ruling class. The state and, by extension, the class in charge of the state is only the servant of the ruling class by reason of its class function.

I argue that the main reason for Poulantzas's adoption of the theory of the equilibrium is the political motivation behind his analysis of fascism. One of his conclusions, as well as one of his primary motivations for this analysis, is to criticise the analysis of fascism by the Third International. Georgi Dimitrov, the leader of the Comintern, had defined fascism as 'the open terrorist dictatorship of the most reactionary, most chauvinistic and most imperialist elements of finance capital'.[49] This definition unequivocally identified the fascist policies with the interests of the capitalist ruling class. According to Poulantzas, the Comintern's analysis was 'economistic', as it reduced the development of the fascist state to an inevitable need of the 'economic' development of capitalism, while underestimating, theoretically and politically, 'the role of the class struggle in the pace and direction of the development of imperialism, which its analyses of fascism demonstrate'.[50] For this reason, Poulantzas tends to overemphasise the relative autonomy of the fascist state to counter the 'economistic' analytical paradigm. The fascist state is relatively autonomous from the politically dominant class—at least more relatively autonomous than the normal liberal-democratic state. This is the determinant characteristic of exceptional state forms.

However, there is a certain dialectics of enhancing and reducing the relative autonomy of the state operating in the fascist dictatorship, which Poulantzas seems to miss. There are certainly elements of the fascist state form that may be considered as enhancing the relative autonomy of the state compared to the liberal-democratic state. These include the recruitment of state officials mainly from the petty bourgeoisie, as well as the lack of an absolute coincidence of certain policies pursued by the Nazi state with interests of the bourgeoisie—a point that is arguable. Nevertheless, as Poulantzas admits, state officials are not exclusively drawn from the bourgeois class, even in the case of the liberal-democratic state.

---

49 Georgi Dimitrov, *The United Front: The Struggle Against Fascism and War* (London: Lawrence and Wishart, 1938), 2.
50 Poulantzas, *Fascism and Dictatorship*, 39. One of the main weaknesses of Poulantzas's argument is that he refers to Comintern as if it is a unified subject without internal contradictions and weaknesses of theoretical analyses influenced by objective conditions in the different socio-political conjunctures. Not only that, but he quotes from works of different parties without clarifying the extent to which the views expressed were repeating or were influenced by the official line of the Comintern; see Poulantzas, *Fascism and Dictatorship*, 36–52.

What is more, there are certainly elements of the dictatorial form that seem to reduce the relative autonomy of the state from the dominant classes. First, the political monopoly of one party and the abolition of all other political parties mean that it is much harder for intra-class antagonisms to be mediated. We saw in Marx's analysis in the 'Eighteenth Brumaire' that a republic is the proper state form to fulfil that function. Second, the open repression against the militant organisation of these classes means that it is easier to expose the class nature of policies that are openly pursued by the fascist state. Third, the abolition of political organisations of the dominated classes makes it harder to mediate the ineradicable class conflict between the two principle classes in capitalist society. These points manifest that there is a delicate dialectics at play between contradictory tendencies that simultaneously enhance and reduce the relative autonomy of the state. Dimitrov seems to pay attention to this dialectic when he comments of the weakness of the ruling bourgeois class, which is exposed in the fascist state, and when he describes the instability of this state form because of the inevitable 'accentuation of class contradictions' that will eventually lead to the explosion of the political monopoly of fascism.[51]

All that being said, and despite the adoption of certain problematic aspects from Gramsci's analysis of Caesarism, there are certain original contributions to the analysis of the dictatorial form as a result of a crisis of hegemony. Poulantzas seems to locate the reason for the fascist solution to the instability of the bourgeoisie's political hegemony and the difficulties in reproducing its rule predominantly through ideological means. According to him, the proliferation of political and class organisations in the interwar period, during the rise of fascism, is evidence of the impotence and instability of bourgeois hegemony.[52] This instability—together with a crisis of party representation as a result of the inability of the bourgeois class to rely on the Social-Democratic Party to represent its strategic interests—eventually led to a radicalisation of the bourgeois parties towards exceptional state forms, such as military dictatorship.[53]

But perhaps the most original element of Poulantzas's analysis is his discussion of the crisis in the dominant ideology as an essential aspect of the crisis of hegemony. The function of ideology of the dominant class in a social formation, according to Poulantzas's structuralist approach, is to ensure the reproduction of capitalist relations by keeping the

---

51 Dimitrov, *The United Front*, 16.
52 Poulantzas, *Fascism and Dictatorship*, 75.
53 Ibid., 74.

oppressed classes politically subject and subordinate.[54] The ideology of the dominant class acts as the 'cement of a social formation' insofar as it succeeds by various means in permeating the 'ideological sub-groupings' of the dominated classes. For instance, the trade-unionist ideology, or the reformist ideology of social-democratic parties, is a form in which 'bourgeois ideology dominates the sub-groupings of working-class ideology insofar as it succeeds in permeating its ideology'.[55]

In 1930s Germany, in the aftermath of the Great Depression, the intensified contradictions of German society resulted in the depreciation of the theretofore dominant ideology of social democracy and in the need for crushing the organised working-class movement, including its 'trade-unionist' elements. Consequently, according to Poulantzas, the ideological sub-ensemble of the petty bourgeoisie rose to prominence.[56] However, it would be even more accurate to speak of bourgeois imperialist ideology permeating the ideology of the middle strata because what Poulantzas calls 'ideological sub-ensemble of the petty bourgeoisie' is actually an amalgam of contradictory elements that includes central aspects of proper imperialist ideology: statist aspects (disguising capital's interest in the interventionist role of the State); anti-juridical aspects (corresponds to interests of big capital and the displacement in imperialist ideology from the juridico-political region to economic technocratism); militarist, nationalist and racist aspects (suits imperialist capital as it corresponds to its colonialist and expansionist interests); and corporatist aspects (which refers to participation in the State through corporations to group all social forces in an authoritarian way, repression of class struggle, subordination of medium capital to big capital).[57]

Nazism as Fascism

I return now to the question we introduced in the first section of this chapter: can the Nazi dictatorship be accurately described as a permanent state of exception? Or is it better described using the Schmittian terms of commissarial or sovereign dictatorship? I argue that approaching the Nazi state form as a type of fascist dictatorship sheds light on the relationship between the different types of dictatorship, as well as on the relationship between the state form and crises of capitalism in its

---

54 Ibid., 76. See also Althusser, *On the Reproduction of Capitalism*.
55 Ibid.
56 Ibid., 251.
57 Ibid.

imperialist stage. This approach focuses primarily on the function of Nazi dictatorship in stabilising and restoring the capitalist social order and structures; on its anti-communist orientation aimed at the crushing of the organisations of the working class; on its imperialistic, expansionist tendencies; on its extreme intolerance towards all oppositional groups expressed through violence and repression; and on its fixation on a plebiscitarily legitimised leader.[58] One of the central points developed here is that a commissarial type of dictatorship is not enough for the reproduction of capitalist social relations in the face of crisis because of the far-reaching nature of the measures necessary to ensure this reproduction. Additionally, the state of exception paradigm cannot explain the dictatorial form of the state because the latter does not correspond to a state of absolute arbitrariness and suspension of the law, but rather to a combination of arbitrariness in certain spheres and legal normality in others.

Beginning with the latter point, we can turn to Ernst Fraenkel's analysis of the 'Dual State'. Fraenkel's central argument was that the Nazi state consists of two constituent and equally necessary elements, namely, a state of pure arbitrariness, which he calls 'prerogative state', and a state of legal normality, which he calls 'normative state'. He argues that the prerogative state is the result of a process through which the National-Socialists 'were able to transform the constitutional and temporary dictatorship (intended to restore public order) into an unconstitutional and permanent dictatorship and to provide the framework of the National-Socialist state with unlimited power'.[59] The task of the prerogative state was to maintain this absolute dictatorship.

Fraenkel argues that Schmitt's theory had been adopted by the Gestapo not just because all legal restrictions to its actions had been removed, but also because its jurisdiction became ever-expanding. With regards to the abolition of legal restrictions, he cites the second law regarding the jurisdiction of the Gestapo (Gesetz uber die Geheime Staatzpolizei, 30 November 1933). This law distinguished between the Gestapo and ordinary police. The acts of the former were not subject to judicial review because the 'State police (Stapo) and the Gestapo were a special police and no particular law providing for the judicial review of its actions existed'.[60] However, gradually the dominant interpretation of the act became such that it exempted from judicial review not just all direct acts of the Gestapo but also: all acts of ordinary police pursuant

---

58 Kershaw, *The Nazi Dictatorship*, 49–50.
59 Fraenkel, *The Dual State*, 5.
60 Ibid., 26.

upon special orders of the Gestapo; all acts of the ordinary police pursuant upon general orders of the Gestapo; as well as all acts of the ordinary police that fall within the jurisdiction of the Gestapo.[61]

Furthermore, the sphere of the prerogative state grew with the increase in the jurisdiction of the Gestapo. This was the result of a blurring, or rather a re-drawing, of the dividing line between political and non-political acts. If the purely political sphere belonged to the prerogative state and could not be subject to review, then the classification of an increasing number of actions as political, rather than private, would enlarge the sphere of the 'prerogative state'. A direct result of this process of extreme politicisation of society was the development of the theory of the 'indirect Communist danger'. This theory was based on an interpretation of the Reichstag Fire Decree. In a decision of 8 December 1935, the criminal division of the Prussian Supreme Court decided that the Decree applied to the members of a Catholic youth organisation.[62] Members of such groups, even if directly opposed to 'atheistic Communism', might indirectly support the Communists by undermining the absolutist nature of the Nazi state.

The rationale behind this theory was that the public expression of private opinion could only serve to encourage persons who believe in or who sympathise with communism, because any public expression of private opinion forms and diffuses the opinion that the Nazi state is not supported by the entirety of the people.[63] This theory of the 'indirect war on Communism' manifests that there is nothing that cannot be classified as political.[64] The prerogative state has the 'Kompetenz-Kompetenz' (i.e. the jurisdiction over jurisdictions): where it requires the political treatment of private and non-state matters, law is suspended; where this is not required, the law operates in normal conditions, in what Fraenkel calls the 'normative state'.[65]

Nevertheless, the expansion of prerogative powers was calculated and served a structural purpose: to reorganise the hegemony of the ruling class and re-stabilise a situation of crisis. For this purpose the state 'arms itself with the means to intervene to do so'.[66] In this context the aforementioned leadership principle was developed. The leadership principle and the Führer's plebiscitary legitimacy served a double purpose. On the one hand they acted as a unifying force against centrifugal

61 Ibid., 27.
62 Ibid., 17.
63 Ibid., 18.
64 Fraenkel, *The Dual State*, 57–58.
65 Ibid., 58.
66 Poulantzas, *Fascism and Dictatorship*, 322.

Reproduction of bourgeois power 67

tendencies, a form accommodating the reconsolidation of German capital. On the other, they provided the system with the legitimacy as well as the fluidity necessary to achieve the re-organisation of hegemony and the stabilisation of a critical situation.[67] Fascism as reconsolidation of the bourgeois regime would be unsuccessful unless it managed to bind to itself strata that socially do not form part of the bourgeois class but that would afford it the inestimable service of anchoring its rule in the people.[68] Plebiscitarianism and the leadership principle were the main legitimating forms to achieve this in the sphere of constitutional law and ideological legitimation of power.

This proves that the elements of arbitrariness of the Nazi dictatorship served a structural purpose. The reproduction of bourgeois rule was conditional upon the re-organisation of its hegemonic position over the dominated classes, as well as the mediation of intra-class conflicts between the ruling class factions. Additionally, restoring the profitability of capital relied on the reproduction of conditions of intensified exploitation. These processes entailed far-reaching changes in the form of exercise of public power.

The German ruling class of the interwar period was not a metaphysical subject that decided *en bloc* or had a single uniform voice. On the contrary, it was replete with conflicting interests that struggled against each other for the best way out of the crisis and for the state form to best accommodate this. Nevertheless, these conflicting groups were unified in the process of dealing with the common enemy (i.e. the working-class movement) for the purpose of promoting a regime of intensified exploitation based on the extraction of absolute surplus value. It was

---

67 The effect of the leadership principle was not confined to constitutional law, but is also encountered in Nazi Germany's labour law. The Nazi state was a 'qualitative total state', indeed, as it set up the German Labour Front, comprised of both employers and employees, no longer called by the old names but now termed 'leaders' and 'followers'. The 'Law for the Organization of National Labour' was issued on 20 January 1934, and under it the German Labour Front was the inclusive organization of German brain and hand workers. See Norman Thomas, 'Labour under the Nazis', 14 *Foreign Affairs*. The German Labour Front was a crucial element of the qualitative total state, as it was the main mechanism of class collaboration. The interests of workers (i.e. the 'followers') were identified with the interests of capitalists (i.e. the 'leaders'). We find here the leadership principle at work in labour law. The 'leader' makes the real decisions, and this fact became undeniable in 1935, when the Reich Chamber of Economics (a bureaucratic organization containing all the employers in Germany, controlled by the Ministry of Economics) joined the Labour Front. The German Labour Front employed the 'Führerprinzip' in the economy and, as the main form of class collaboration, provided the Nazi regime with the social power base necessary for its reproduction.
68 Scheuerman, *Carl Schmitt: The End of Law*, 122.

68 Reproduction of bourgeois power

for this reason, ultimately, that the dictatorial form of the Nazi state came into being: to consolidate the bourgeois rule and facilitate the intensification of exploitation.

As far as the intra-class conflicts are concerned, it has been argued that during the interwar period the German businesses were divided into two main groups: those that demanded a policy of free trade, such as the textile and pharmaceutical industries, and those that tended towards protectionism, such as the industries of agriculture, iron and steel.[69] By the end of the 1920s the leading role had fallen to the former, the so-called new industries (i.e. the large-scale finishing ones, such as the big chemical firms, the heavy machine manufacturers and the electro-industry), while the iron and steel industries had slipped into a subordinate position. This was hardly to the liking of the latter whose aims for realising the full productive potential of their plant could only be served by a determined policy of re-armament.[70]

The process of concentration of the decisive elements of German monopoly capital in a new grouping of interests is described by Alfred Sohn-Rethel. According to his analysis, the establishment of fascism in Germany in January 1933 was a result, on the one hand, of the political victory of the dysfunctional groups of big and small businesses over the financially sound parts of the German economy. By the end of 1932, the near entirety of German finance capital had coalesced on a policy bent on violent expansion and war.[71] Germany's production capacities were far too large for its own narrow market. Hence, the need for a larger internal market arose. This was expressed in the Nazi theory of the 'Living Space', but also in the expansion of the armament policies.

On the other hand, the victory of one group of businesses over the other was underlined by the *common interest* in suppressing wages and increasing the number of working hours.[72] A reversion of the capitalist mode of production *from the relative to the absolute surplus value extraction* (i.e. intensification of exploitation by increase in the number of working hours and drop in real wages) was necessitated for the German capital not to spiral downwards into inescapable crisis. Of course, the attack on the workers' rights and the welfare state and the pursuing of policies directed at the lowering of labour costs did not begin with Hitler's rise to power. Ever since September 1926, the German

---

69 Alfred Sohn-Rethel, *Economy and Class Structure of German Fascism* (London: Process Press Ltd, 1987), 16.
70 Ibid., 46.
71 Ibid., 89.
72 Ibid., 55.

industrialists had shown that they could no longer afford the gains won by the working class between 1918 and 1923, by issuing a statement attacking the 'too generous distribution of social benefits' and calling for a 'reduction of the burden of taxation' to 'restore the profitability of the economy'.[73] Just weeks after the Wall Street crash, the League of German Industry called for the welfare state to be 'adapted to the limits of economic sustainability', decreeing 'unjustified and immoral abuse' of social security benefits because in their eyes the economic crisis had been caused by a bloated welfare state, high wages and short working hours.[74]

This shows that the Weimar welfare form could not accommodate the new conditions of intensified exploitation. The state had to shed its skin and assume a different form. What German finance capital needed above all was *to break out of the falling rate of profit by the only means in existence that depended neither on other capitalist powers nor on the world market (i.e. a forced raising of the rate of surplus value by the slashing of the workers' wages)*.[75] This was the economic need that was met by Hitler's policies, which consisted of a systematic lowering of wages. The millions of unemployed were gradually re-employed at rates of pay no higher, or hardly so, than their unemployment benefit. 'Work for all, not wealth for all', as the Nazis expressed it after they had smashed the trades unions. The great mass of financially weak firms welcomed Hitler's economic 'revival' methods because through them they could escape the more or less acute danger of bankruptcy.[76]

But the aggressive policies necessary to achieve this systematic lowering of wages involved a sustained attack on workers' rights, which were safeguarded in the Weimar Constitution. The leaders of German industries were well aware that the policy they were compelled to pursue in the economic crisis, with the attacks on all sections of the workers, including those who had gained by the previous social legislation, inevitably meant the weakening of the basis of social democracy. These policies *could not be realised* in conditions of intensified class struggle and growing militancy of the workers, *unless* the bourgeois elite was able to smash not only the proletarian political organisations but also the mass basis appropriate to the previous system of control through relative

---

73 Ibid., 8.
74 Marcel Bois, 'Hitler Wasn't Inevitable', in *Jacobin*, 25 November 2015, available at www.jacobinmag.com/2015/11/nuremberg-trials-hitler-goebbels-himmler-german-communist-social-democrats/.
75 Sohn-Rethel, *Economy and Class Structure of German Fascism*, 89 (emphasis added).
76 Ibid., 39.

surplus value production, namely, the trade unions and social democracy. The best analysis of the reasons that necessitated the change from the Weimar to the Nazi form was made before the Reichstag on 21 May 1935 by Adolf Hitler himself:

> In order to assure the functioning of the national economy it became *necessary to arrest the movement of wages and prices*. It was also *necessary to stop all interferences which are not in accord with the higher interests of our national economy*, i.e. it was *imperative to eliminate all class organisations which pursued their own policies with regard to wages and prices*. The destruction of the class-struggle organisations of employers as well as of employees required the analogous *elimination of those political parties* which were financed and supporter by those interest groups. This process, in its turn, caused the introduction of a new constructive and effective 'living constitution' and the refoundation of Reich and State.[77]

As former Nazi official Albert Krebs described in his memoirs: 'Not all capitalists were particularly enthusiastic about the Nazis, but their scepticism was relative and ended as soon as it became clear that Hitler was the only person capable of destroying the labour movement'.[78] The Nazi state form and the Nazi economic model formed a unified yet contradictory whole. These new economic and political forms corresponded to the intensification of capitalist contradictions after the capitalist crisis and to the objective need to restore the profitability of German enterprises and to advance to a new political system. The new state form would achieve this by crushing the working-class movement and re-organising the hegemony of the ruling class over the dominated classes.

The Nazi state form reproduced the foundational conditions of the capitalist relations (i.e. private property of the means of production) in the face of rising class and intra-class contradictions. To do so, apart from introducing a variety of authoritarian elements, it had to preserve and reproduce structures that ensured the calculability necessary for the functioning of a capitalist economy. This function is captured accurately in Fraenkel's notion of the 'normative state'. The existence of a normative state was essential, because it protected the institutions of private property, contract and private enterprise, which were still the basis of

---

77 Quoted in Fraenkel, *The Dual State*, 187 (emphasis added).
78 Albert Krebs, *The Infancy of Nazism: The Memoirs of Ex-Gauleiter Albert Krebs* (London: New Viewpoints, 1976).

German society.⁷⁹ The regulation of the Nazi state's future activities by legal rules was appropriate insofar as it satisfied the requirements of the 'constructive forces of the nation', namely, the interests of the 'leaders of private business'. In the name of legal certainty and calculability, the courts saw that the institutions and principles of the capitalist order (such as freedom of enterprise, sanctity of contracts, private property, the right of the entrepreneur to control labour, regulation of unfair competition, regulation of patent, trademark rights, legal protection for interest agreements, etc.) were maintained.⁸⁰

Fraenkel's analysis comes to supplement and enhance Franz Neumann's analysis of the Nazi state form. In his *Behemoth*, Neumann argues that the emergence of monopoly capitalism necessarily entails arbitrary power that directly serves the large-scale capitalist firm.⁸¹ This is also highlighted by Poulantzas, who claims that 'law in the fascist State has the same basic characteristics as in the interventionist State form' of monopoly capitalism. Even if it is accepted that monopoly capitalism is often more discretionary than its competitive capitalist predecessor, and that the intensified contradictions that accommodate this highest stage of capitalism necessitate a move towards more authoritarian forms of exercise of public power, this arbitrariness presupposes the preservation of some minimal measure of legal calculability, for both these elements in the last instance serve the reproduction of the capitalist relations of production. Thus, according to Poulantzas, National Socialism basically kept the law of the Weimar Republic, which was the first juridical system in an imperialist country to make the turn to the stage of monopoly capitalism.⁸²

The view that National Socialism corresponded to a state of pure arbitrariness or a permanent state of exception is mistaken. Capitalism, even in its monopoly stage, cannot do without some measure of traditional legal calculability. The prerogative state, the main site for Nazi legal arbitrariness, is functioning alongside the normative state. It intervenes in the latter whenever it considers appropriate. It is legally unlimited vis-à-vis the normative state: when politically desirable, court decisions are simply discarded or revised.⁸³ But, in Fraenkel's

---

79 Ibid., 186.
80 Ibid., 73.
81 'Legal standards of conduct (blanket clauses) serve the monopolist. . . . Not only is rational law unnecessary for him, it is often a fetter upon the full development of his productive force, or more frequently, upon the limitations that he may desire; rational law, after all serves also to protect the weak'; see Neumann, *Behemoth*, 447.
82 Poulantzas, *Fascism and Dictatorship*, 323.
83 Scheuerman, *Carl Schmitt: The End of Law*, 91.

interpretation a significant number of more or less traditional legal proceedings are left untouched by National Socialism.[84] To the extent that the Nazi state form reproduces the main conditions of capitalism (private property, contract, private enterprise) the scope of the prerogative state is limited. The reproduction of capitalist relations of production was the content, purpose and absolute limit of Nazi state form.

We can draw the conclusion that the normal and the exceptional forms of exercise of public power are different but not incompatible. A fundamental necessity underlies both norm and exception: that of reproducing a regime of power, property and production relations. The ordinary function of the rule of law, which safeguards this regime, is conditional upon the non-occurrence of the always existent and imminent danger, which Schmitt calls the 'ever-present possibility of conflict'. In the case of an existential crisis of capitalist rule and the capitalist state, a dictatorial form may be necessitated. What is more, in the imperialist stage of capitalism, a constitutional dictatorship, such as the one prescribed in Article 48 of the Weimar Republic, is not enough to reproduce the bourgeois state and rule, because of the far-reaching nature of the measures that are necessary for this.

A capitalist crisis in the monopoly stage of capitalism may threaten the reproduction of the bourgeois state and rule on many levels, affecting both the class contradictions and the intra-class balance of powers. This means that a radical re-orientation of core internal and foreign policies involving a series of measures and alterations of the legal order is necessary for this reproduction. This makes sense if one thinks about the previous regime (i.e. the welfare state of the Weimar Republic) whereby the working-class movement had won vital concessions through bloody struggles during the German Revolution—which had to be eradicated. The above analysis showed that this process involves not just a temporary suspension of civil liberties, but a series of measures of administrative law, labour law, etc. The commissarial dictatorship turned into a 'sovereign' one and established a dictatorial form of state.

---

84 An example of this is provided by the estates system of the Nazi regime: 'The most important attempt of private business to free itself from the intervention of the police authorities is to be found in the estate system.... The symbol "estates" merely serves as a protective ideological colouring adopted by business-men to protect themselves from the interference of the Prerogative State. Their protection is simply this—that matters within the jurisdiction of the estates are de facto outside the police power'; Fraenkel, *The Dual State*, 97.

4 Dictatorship and the supersession of the bourgeois state

In the previous chapters we discussed the role of the institution, the different types, as well as the discourse of dictatorship in the processes of consolidating and reproducing the rule of the bourgeois class. The social function of dictatorship was associated with the dialectical transformation of the bourgeoisie from revolutionary agent in Europe to new ruling class and agent of counter-revolution. But before it became the emblematic institution for the counter-revolution, dictatorship was associated with the revolutionary processes, in fact, with the more radical elements of these processes, as we saw in the discussion of the Committee of Public Safety and the French National Convention in the context of the French Revolution. Notably, Jean-Paul Marat, the 'friend of the people' and voice of the sans-culottes (the working-class and poorest strata of revolutionary France), had openly proposed a dictatorship to defend the revolution against its enemies.[1]

After the counter-revolutionary turn of the bourgeoisie, the revolutionary potential of the concept of dictatorship was not lost. The new revolutionary social force, the proletariat, would also organise its struggle for power around a concept of dictatorship. This chapter discusses the concept of dictatorship in Marxist discourse and the theory of the dictatorship of the proletariat in the struggle for supersession of the bourgeois state. It starts by examining the meaning of the term in the works of the classics of Marxism, namely Marx, Engels and Lenin. It continues with a discussion of the need to reopen the debate on the Marxist concept of dictatorship, which seems to have been pushed aside for several decades after the theoretical victory of Eurocommunism in Western Europe. To this end, the last two sections of the chapter examine the relationship between dictatorship and democracy in the Marxist discourse, as well as the significance of the Marxist conception

1 Draper, *The Dictatorship of the Proletariat*, 23–25.

of dictatorship for grasping the relationship between juridico-political and socio-economic processes.

Throughout the chapter the implications of these conceptions and processes with regards to the law are discussed. An examination of the Marxist concept of 'dictatorship' presupposes a deep engagement with the relationship between law and revolution. The role of law in the process of socio-economic change is another issue that takes centre stage. Historically, the concept of dictatorship of the proletariat has been central in the discussion of the relationship between bourgeois law and socialist law: the existence (or not) of the latter and the withering away (or not) of the former in the revolutionary transformation of capitalist society. Of course these questions are politically sensitive but they are also questions that have sparked wide and deep academic debates. This chapter proceeds with an overview of these debates in tight connection with the concept of dictatorship on the basis of a firm conviction that there are very good reasons for revisiting these debates, not the least of which are the intensifying contradictions of capitalism globally, as well as the failure of Eurocommunist theories to interpret these contradictions and provide the working class and popular strata with the means to contest the capitalist regime of power, property and production relations.

Dictatorship as class rule

With regards to the appearance and use of the concept of dictatorship in the works of Marx and Engels, there is a leading authority—Hal Draper and his work, *Karl Marx's Theory of Revolution*, and especially Volume 3 of this work, *The Dictatorship of the Proletariat*,[2] as well as his follow-up work, *The Dictatorship of the Proletariat from Marx to Lenin*.[3] Draper, in an excellent scholarly work, pinpoints thirteen loci in Marx and Engels's writing where the concept of dictatorship was used. He identifies three periods when this concept appeared: from 1850 to 1852 (i.e. the post-revolutionary period after the upheaval of 1848–1849); from 1871 to 1875 (i.e. the post-revolutionary period after the Paris Commune); and a third period after 1875 in the work of Engels alone, as a 'sort of echo from 1875'.[4]

In his work, Draper proves in a very convincing and scholarly manner that the concept of dictatorship in Marxian work refers to the 'class

---

2 Draper, *Karl Marx's Theory of Revolution*.
3 Draper, *The Dictatorship of the Proletariat*.
4 Ibid., 23.

nature of political power' rather than to 'special governmental forms'.[5] In other words, the concept of dictatorship in Marx and Engels refers not just to the political form of exercise of power, but to the wider issue of class rule and socio-economic power. This is a very important point, as it already takes the analysis of dictatorship beyond the narrow scope defined by classical and modern bourgeois thinkers. The Marxian conception of dictatorship takes into account the juridico-political form together with the socio-economic content expressed in this form. For instance, the concept 'dictatorship of the bourgeoisie' refers not only to bourgeois dictatorial regimes or to the rule of the bourgeoisie by martial law, but in general to the mechanisms through which the bourgeois class exercises its political power through the state apparatus (repressive and ideological in the sense discussed in the previous chapters), even in the context of a liberal democracy.

Contrary to Draper's claim that dictatorship was used by Marx only in connection with the Blanquist and Jacobin revolutionary currents as a means to re-educate them,[6] I argue that the reasons for the use of this specific concept are to be found not so much in Marx's 'political opportunism' but in the traits of the concept itself. For instance, to refer to the class rule of the proletariat, Marx opts for class dictatorship more often than he does for class despotism. The characteristics of the two concepts are to account for this. Despotism signifies absolute power and oppression, whereas dictatorship signifies power that is limited temporarily and on the basis of a strict mandate. The former is incompatible with democracy while the latter is compatible with democratic rule. Therefore, the proletariat may arguably rule as a dictator but not as a despot. The rule of the proletariat is temporarily limited because, during its rule, the proletariat builds the conditions for the abolition of rule altogether. Thus, the element of transitionality is crucial for the adoption of this concept; so is the commissarial character of dictatorship. The rule of the proletariat is exercised for the achievement of a specific goal (i.e. the socialist construction and the transition to communism).

Dictatorship of the proletariat means the rule of the proletariat, but not in an abstract way. Marx's theoretical work did not operate in one-sided abstractions but is known for its capacity to dialectically unite the abstract and the concrete.[7] The question here is: can a workers' state

5 Ibid., 32.
6 Ibid., 26.
7 E.V. Ilyenkov, *The Dialectics of the Abstract and the Concrete in Marx's Capital* (Delhi: Aakar Books, 2008).

be established by winning elections for the bourgeois parliament? Can the workers' rule be established without smashing the bourgeois state? Marx and Engels had clearly expressed their views on these questions, and I argue that these views amount to a Marxian theory of dictatorship. The Marxist concept of dictatorship refers to the issue of the societal content of the state (i.e. the class character of political power). But it also refers to the process of *establishing* the rule of the proletariat, by organising the proletariat in an independent political party and smashing the bourgeois state, according to Marx and Engels's revolutionary theory.

Marx's revolutionary standpoint was crucial for the adoption of the concept of dictatorship. His thesis in the 'Eighteenth Brumaire' that 'all revolutions had perfected the [state] machine instead of smashing it' left no doubt as to the tasks of the proletarian revolution. This thesis applied his eleventh thesis on Feuerbach ('Philosophers have hitherto only interpreted the world in various ways; the point is to change it') to the field of political and revolutionary theory. To claim, as Draper does,[8] that the Paris Commune's lack of 'dictatorial trappings' is evidence of Marx's indifference to the ways of capturing state power is to negate Marx's whole analysis of the Paris Commune. Marx seems to be criticising the limits of the Commune and is definitely problematising on the question of how proletarian rule is established—thus developing a theory of dictatorship.

It is true that, in terms of political form, the Paris Commune cannot be characterised as a dictatorial regime, at least in the sense described in the previous chapters. Its guiding principle was radical democracy: the extension of representation from parliament to the bureaucracy, the judiciary and the army; universalisation of suffrage; strict accountability of delegates to their electors and revocability at short notice; abolition of the division of powers between legislature and executive in favour of legislative dominance; abolition of internal hierarchies within the state officialdom; popular organisation independent of the state; replacement of the army by the 'people armed'.[9] These were the characteristics of the political form of the Commune.

The undeniably democratic nature of the political form of the Paris Commune was precisely one of the main foci of Marx's elaboration on the relationship between the democratic forms of government and the practical needs of the revolution. The form of the Paris Commune was

---

8 Draper, *The Dictatorship of the Proletariat*, 30.
9 Robert Fine, *Democracy and the Rule of Law* (Coldwell: The Blackburn Press, 2002), 127.

democratic and its content was the rule of labour over capital. But the main question is the compatibility of form and content. In his letter to Kugelmann (of 12 April 1871) Marx suggests that if the 'comrades of Paris' are defeated, 'only their "good nature" will be to blame', because 'they should have marched at once on Versailles'.[10] Instead the 'Central Committee surrendered its power too soon, to make way for the Commune' and its democratic election.[11] This suggests that Marx clearly identified a tension between form and content, democracy and proletarian rule. The Marxian and Marxist concept of dictatorship concerns itself with this tension between a fuller democratic form of proletarian rule and the reproduction of this rule.

This tension shaped the fate of the international working-class movement in the early twentieth century. In 1903 the Second Congress of the Russian Social Democratic Party took place. This is best known for the Bolshevik–Menshevik split. In his contribution, Georgi Plekhanov suggested that the basic principle of democracy (i.e. *Salus populi suprema lex* [the welfare of the people is the highest law]), when translated into the language of the revolutionary, changes into *Salus revolutionis suprema lex* [the success of the revolution is the highest law].[12] This essentially means that, 'if it were necessary for the success of the revolution to restrict the effect of one or another democratic principle, it would be criminal to hesitate at such a restriction'.[13] Plekhanov continued by saying that, 'hypothetically it is conceivable that we, Social-Democrats, may have occasion to come out against universal suffrage'.[14]

The above statement by Plekhanov seems to further develop Marx's own elaboration on the dialectical unity of form and content of the Paris Commune. Establishing a fuller democratic form while suppressing the counter-revolution was a pressing problem of the rising, militant working-class movement. Marx and Engels's positions on this issue

10 Karl Marx, 'Marx to Ludwig Kugelmann. 12 April', in Karl Marx and Friedrich Engels, *Collected Works: Volume 44* (London: Lawrence and Wishart, 2010), 131.
11 Ibid.
12 Draper, *The Dictatorship of the Proletariat*, 70.
13 Ibid.
14 Ibid., 71. In 1903 'Social-Democrats' was the name used for the majority of the working-class parties (i.e. for both the revolutionary and reformist currents of the working-class movement). 'Social-democracy' had not yet crystallized into a concept to describe the bourgeois reformist forces operating in the movement. The split between the Bolsheviks and Mensheviks was followed by another split in the international working-class movement between the Social-Democratic parties, which in the context of the First World War supported their national bourgeoisies, and the communist parties, which followed the Bolshevik line of proletarian internationalism and revolution.

were carried forward and developed by theorists such as Plekhanov, Lenin and Luxemburg in the late nineteenth and early twentieth centuries. Engels himself had emphasised the authoritarian nature of a revolution 'whereby one part of the population imposes its will upon the other part by means of rifles, bayonets and cannon'.[15] In the same spirit as Marx in his letter to Kugelmann, he suggested that the Paris Commune could be reproached for not having used 'the terror which its arms inspire' freely enough.[16] This view, which refers to the revolutionary process of establishing a workers' state, is echoed in Lenin's definition of dictatorship. In his 1906 pamphlet, 'The Victory of the Cadets and the Tasks of the Workers' Party', Lenin defined dictatorship as 'unlimited power based on force, and not on law'.[17]

It is crucial—and quite challenging—to grasp that Lenin's definition of dictatorship refers not so much to the form of government, but rather to the source of authority of the workers' state. The source of authority of proletarian rule cannot be a law of the bourgeois state. This means that, according to Lenin, the socialist construction cannot be the result of a legislative reform in the bourgeois parliament. The workers' state establishes its own rules, its own laws, its own standards, which are not based on bourgeois laws and political institutions. The Leninist concept of dictatorship refers to the totality of social relations and processes (e.g. the process of socialist construction and the development of socialist relations of production). Lenin's conception is thus wider than the bourgeois formalist conception of dictatorship and extends to processes of socio-economic change and the elimination of social contradictions towards communism.

A couple of final remarks are pertinent here before we move on to discuss these features of the Marxist concept of dictatorship that distinguish it from the bourgeois formalist concept discussed thus far. First, the issue of the source of authority of a regime should not be confused with lawlessness. A proletarian revolution is not a state of chaos or anomie; it gives rise to new law. But this new law and new regime is not

---

15 Friedrich Engels, 'On Authority', in Karl Marx and Friedrich Engels, *Collected Works: Volume 23* (London: Lawrence and Wishart, 2010), 425.
16 Ibid.
17 V.I. Lenin, 'The Victory of the Cadets and the Tasks of the Workers' Party', in *Collected Works: Volume 10* (Moscow: Progress Publishers, 1974), 216. The Cadets were constitutional democrats; their official name was the 'Party of the People's Freedom'. Composed of liberals from the propertied classes, this was the party of political reform that formed the first Provisional Government of February 1917. As the revolution became a social-economic revolution, the Cadets grew more conservative; see John Reed, *Ten Days that Shook the World* (London: Penguin, 1977), 18.

authorised by bourgeois parliament. To claim that the dictatorship of the proletariat is unlimited power based on force and not on law means that the rule of the proletariat has no bourgeois legal basis, but is directly backed by the armed force of the people.

The view that equates Lenin's conception of dictatorship with sheer power and the arbitrariness of an anti-democratic regime is false. It is countered by Lenin's well-documented defence of the democratic form of the proletarian dictatorship. In his 'State and Revolution', Lenin discusses the principles of electivity, revocability and working-man's wage as principles of a fuller democracy than bourgeois parliamentary democracy. Elsewhere, he argued that the issue of disenfranchising the bourgeoisie should not be regarded 'from an absolute point of view, because it is theoretically quite conceivable that the dictatorship of the proletariat may suppress the bourgeoisie at every step without disenfranchising them'.[18] The Soviet political form would not be the sole model for all countries because the transition from capitalism to communism is 'bound to yield a tremendous abundance and variety of political forms'.[19] However, this also means that the form of a workers' state will not necessarily be only democratic. 'Abundance and variety of political forms' means that a situation of crisis might also necessitate the adoption of a dictatorial form. After all, state power entails violence and repression for the reproduction of a regime of power, property and production relations. Nevertheless, this is far from negating the democratic essence of the dictatorship of the proletariat, as we shall see in the following sections.

Reopening the debate on Marxist 'dictatorship'

Reopening the debate on 'dictatorship of the proletariat' might *prima facie* appear 'outlandish'. It did appear outlandish to Grahame Lock in 1977, when he wrote the 'Introduction' to Etienne Balibar's *On the Dictatorship of the Proletariat*.[20] Balibar's work was a defence of this principle in the context of the 22nd Congress of the French Communist Party, which decided to eliminate it from its programme and substitute for it the objective of a 'democratic' road to socialism. The debate on the dictatorship of the proletariat has appeared outlandish in Western

---

18 V.I. Lenin, 'Report on the Party Programme, March 19', in *Collected Works: Volume 29*, (Moscow: Progress Publishers, 1974), 184.
19 V.I. Lenin, 'The State and Revolution', in *Collected Works: Volume 25* (Moscow: Progress Publishers, 1974), 418.
20 Grahame Lock, 'Introduction', in Etienne Balibar, *On the Dictatorship of the Proletariat* (London: NLB, 1977), 7.

80 The Supersession of the bourgeois state

Marxist theory and political strategy, ever since the gradual ideological victory of the Eurocommunist current—a current that pursued a reformist strategy by arguing for a parliamentary road to socialism and the abandonment of the revolutionary characteristics of workers' parties. This was true in the 1970s when this debate took place outside the boundaries set by the dominant ideology and thus outside the boundaries of 'common sense'. This is even truer nowadays when bourgeois ideology has all but triumphed and 'common sense' pejoratively equates Marxist dictatorship with totalitarianism.

In 2019, after the complete transformation of Syriza—the intellectual and political offspring of the Greek Communist Party of the Interior and perhaps the last major exponent of Eurocommunism in Europe—into a bourgeois party of social-democracy, which itself followed the reduction to insignificance of the former major exponents of this current, such as the Italian Communist Party, the Communist Party of France and the Communist Party of Spain, the ultimate failure of Eurocommunism in providing the toiling classes with the analytical tools to draw an emancipatory strategy is an undeniable fact. This makes it necessary for any attempt at reloading a Marxist critique of capitalism to reassess the concept of Marxist dictatorship. To do this, one has to examine the Eurocommunist current's attack on the revolutionary elements of Marxist thought, which was carried out on the basis of the following antitheses: reform and revolution, democracy and dictatorship, legality and illegality. An exhaustive analysis of the policies of these parties and the major theorists (like Gramsci or Poulantzas) who influenced them lies outside the scope of this book.[21] Nevertheless,

---

21 For an extensive analysis of the current of Eurocommunism, see Kostas Skolarikos, *Eurocommunism: Theory and Strategy in Favour of Capital* (in Greek) (Athens: Synchroni Epochi, 2016). For a criticism of this current—among others—see Ellen Meiksins Wood, *The Retreat from Class* (London: Verso, 1986). According to Wood, the two pillars of Eurocommunist theory are its analysis of the state and its analysis of class. In fact, the latter seems to determine the former. The view that the state is 'penetrable' to popular struggles and can be transformed from within is determined by the critical question of the agency of social change. Eurocommunist theory displaces the working class from its privileged role as the agent of revolutionary change and diminishes the function of class struggle as the principal motor of social transformation (see Wood, *The Retreat from Class*, 21). In Poulantzas's formulation, relations of exploitation cease to be decisive, and the opposition between capital and labour is displaced by the opposition between 'monopolistic forces' and 'popular masses' (see Wood, *The Retreat from Class*, 31). This displacement presupposes, and is also the result of, a redefinition of the state as well as of the working class. The working class is redefined and reduced to minute proportions so that any strategy for social change that ignores the necessity of a wide popular alliance appears naive. Wood argues that this redefinition of the working class by Poulantzas is based on a misreading of

The Supersession of the bourgeois state 81

a brief discussion of Poulantzas's state theory will prove beneficial for understanding the Eurocommunist opposite to Marxist 'dictatorship' and why the latter needs to be revisited.

To begin with, there is an apparent contradiction in Poulantzas's analysis. A part of it remains Marxist, following the Marxist method of analysis, but the majority of conclusions arrived at seems to be superimposed. For instance, at one point Poulantzas seems to grasp and accurately describe the meaning of the phrase 'every State is a class "dictatorship"'. He explains this as meaning that 'the existence of law or legality has never forestalled any kind of barbarism or despotism'. He adds that 'even the most dictatorial of States is never devoid of law'. Thus, he concludes that 'every State is organized as a single functional order of legality and illegality, of legality shot through with illegality'.[22] This dialectics of legality and illegality, norm and exception, consent and force, is a rather accurate depiction of the issues discussed in the previous chapters concerning the State's role in the reproduction of class rule.

Nevertheless, later on in the same work, Poulantzas goes on by characterising the Marxist theory of dictatorship and the positions that this entails (such as 'every State is a class State'; 'all political domination is a species of class dictatorship'; 'the capitalist State is a State of the bourgeoisie') as 'dogmatic banalities' that are incapable of advancing research by a single inch, because they cannot account for the differential forms and historical transformations of the capitalist State.[23] Of course, this accusation of reductionism contradicts Lenin's view, which was discussed in the previous section. 'Tremendous abundance and variety of political forms' of a class dictatorship means precisely that the form is not neglected and one form is not reduced to the other. On the contrary, Marxist dictatorship emphasises that the class nature of political rule is crucial for understanding the concrete processes that determine the historically specific juridico-political forms. The Marxist

---

Marx (see Wood, *The Retreat from Class*, 37) that stubbornly rejects the inclusion of new wage-earning groups (i.e. white-collar workers in sectors that have been increasingly proletarianised) to the working class (see Wood, *The Retreat from Class*, 35). Poulantzas's refusal to accept the theories that 'dissolve' these strata into the working class betrays a metaphysical and static conception of class situations that ignores the process of class development. Refusing to accept these elements within the ranks of the working class means that the working class in the Western world is reduced to minute proportions and cannot rise to power by itself, but only through alliances with the petty bourgeoisie and elements of the bourgeoisie, hence the need for redefining a strategy towards the state, as well as redefining the state itself.
22 Poulantzas, *State, Power, Socialism*, 85.
23 Ibid., 124–125.

concept of 'dictatorship' captures the unity of form and content and does not elevate the form to the determinant factor, separated from class struggle and relations of production.

Poulantzas's accusation of reductionism betrays a formalist understanding of Marxist 'dictatorship' that fails to grasp how this concept is wider than the bourgeois concept of dictatorship *qua* political form. His view reproduces the bourgeois criticism along the lines of the opposition 'democracy versus dictatorship'. Poulantzas's formalism is impermissible from a Marxist standpoint, yet his position flows directly from his definition of the state and his views on the political strategy of the 'left'. According to Poulantzas, the capitalist state should not be regarded as an intrinsic entity but rather as 'a relationship of forces'. Like capital, the state expresses in a necessarily specific form 'the material condensation of such a relationship among classes and class fractions'.[24] Poulantzas contradicts the Marxist view of the state as a mechanism that ensures the reproduction of class rule and the conditions of capitalist production. According to him, the State itself is permeated by class struggle. Its nature is not established, it is not a bourgeois state. Its nature is the outcome of class struggle that is carried out internally because the state is a relation. The state, then, is 'up for grabs'. The bureaucratic machinery, the repressive and ideological apparatuses, can be won over to the proletarian side through a long process of struggle, gradually.

This conception of the state is essential for Poulantzas's politics of a 'democratic socialism'. The political strategy of Eurocommunist parties, the 'democratic road to socialism', is, according to Poulantzas, 'a long process, in which the struggle of the popular masses does not seek to create an effective dual power parallel and external to the State, but brings itself to bear on the internal contradictions of the State'.[25] In this process the state is not 'crushed', but rather 'transformed from within', and the 'relationship of forces within the state apparatuses' is modified. Of course, winning the bourgeois elections and carrying out the struggle within the state by enacting 'socialist' measures is a (necessary, albeit not adequate) part of this process. As Ellen Meiksins Wood puts it, Eurocommunist parties offer themselves both as 'parties of struggle' and as 'parties of government' that, by achieving electoral victories, can penetrate the bourgeois-democratic state, transform it and implant the conditions for socialism.[26]

---

24 Ibid., 128–129.
25 Ibid., 257.
26 Wood, *Retreat from Class*, 19.

I argue that the main problem with this analysis is that it seems blind to the aspect of violence. The repressive elements of the state are not purely decorative. As we saw in the previous chapter, there is a historical reason why the intensified contradictions in interwar Europe resulted in the proliferation of dictatorial regimes. Poulantzas seems to pay no attention to the well-known—and repeated by him in earlier works—Marxist thesis that the exercise of State violence is not neutral or arbitrary, but always class orientated. If power is a political relation, then it is a relation between dominant and dominated classes; a relation that is mediated through violence. Property and relations of production in a capitalist social formation are mediated through violence. In the last instance, violence will make its appearance, as it happened in Chile in 1973. It is for this reason that Marx stressed the importance of class struggle leading to the dictatorship of the proletariat. The revolutionary aspect is essential to Marx's analysis. His dictatorship of the proletariat makes no sense without the element of armed workers.

On the contrary, Poulantzas's analysis parts ways with Marxism because of its limited and superficial recognition of the issue of violence and counter-revolution,[27] as well as its overestimation of the 'socialist' potential of bourgeois institutions. Poulantzas's analysis reproduces the bourgeois, formalist critique of the Soviet regime along the lines of an opposition between 'statism' and 'rank-and-file democracy'. Between these two traditions, the 'statist' tradition is the 'anti-democratic' one, which is represented by Lenin, Stalin and the Third International.[28] Poulantzas attributes the statism of the U.S.S.R. to Lenin's 'reduction of representative democracy and political freedoms to a simple emanation of the bourgeoisie' and his strategy of frontal attack on bourgeois parliamentary institutions.[29] In essence, he argues that the theory of the dictatorship of the proletariat is the reason behind statism and authoritarianism in the U.S.S.R. The revolutionary demands for abolition of bourgeois representation and a fuller democracy based on new proletarian institutions resulted in the exact opposite, according to Poulantzas. The reason lies in the exclusive reliance on council democracy and the complete elimination of representative democracy, which eventually led to the crippling of political life and its replacement by bureaucracy. 'Without general elections, without unrestricted freedom of press and assembly, without a free struggle of opinion, life dies out

---

27 Poulantzas, *State, Power, Socialism*, 263.
28 Ibid., 251.
29 Ibid., 252.

in every public institution'. Life in the soviets also becomes increasingly crippled, and only bureaucracy remains as the active element.[30]

Is this an accurate depiction of what took place following the October Revolution? Would a process involving the assimilation of elements of council democracy within the organisational structure of representative democracy be more successful in promoting the workers' goals? Let us briefly address these questions by looking at the fate of the institution of workers' councils in interwar Germany, where the working-class movement followed the 'democratic' road to socialism as set out by the Social Democratic Party after the defeat of the German Revolution of 1918.

The role of the Soviets or workers' councils in the struggle for proletarian rule was crucial in the fierce debates of the Second International during and immediately after the First World War, the establishment of the first workers' state in Russia in 1917 and the pan-European revolutionary movement that followed it. Alongside questions such as 'reform or revolution', 'dictatorship of the proletariat or evolutionary road to socialism', the question of the soviets 'as state political institutions' (i.e. forms of proletarian government) or 'institutions of economic class struggle' (i.e. instruments of class collaboration) rose to prominence. In Russia, the soviets became the exemplary institution of the democratic form of the 'dictatorship of the proletariat'. On the contrary, in Germany after the defeat of the Revolution, the workers' councils were recognised in the bourgeois Weimar Constitution drafted under the influence of social-democratic theory.

Article 165 of the Weimar Constitution provided for a system of councils. Its call to all citizens 'to participate in the regulation of wages and conditions of employment' practically meant that a system of councils would be formed: industrial councils and workers' councils. The goal for these industrial councils was to put an end to the unilateral decision-making power of management in production matters. In this manner they were an essential aspect of extending 'democracy' to economic relations. But their function would be restricted to the economic sphere. They would not act to replace parliament; they would be organs of economic, not political, democracy.[31] In addition to the industrial councils, workers' councils would be formed to represent the workers' interests at the workplace level.[32]

---

30 Ibid., 253.
31 Ruth Dukes, 'Constitutionalizing Employment Relations: Sinzheimer, Kahn-Freund, and the Role of Labour Law', 35 *Journal of Law and Society*, 341, 349.
32 Ibid.

On this basis, the limitations of the 'parliamentary road to socialism' are manifested in two ways. The first concerns the role of workers' councils in bourgeois society, which is limited to economic affairs. Industrial and workers' councils are not to act as political institutions or vehicles of radicalization. This is their fundamental difference from Russian Soviets or the short-lived workers' councils of the 1919 Revolution. Article 165 councils are not autonomous, but merely parties to negotiations, members of a 'community'. The defeat of the 1918 revolutions was reflected in a council system based on class collaboration, which was entirely different from the working-class institutions, where the slogan 'all power to the soviets!' (Вся власть советам!) was used to oppose the bourgeois government of Kerensky. The second point concerns the non-implementation of several aspects of the economic constitution. Statutory provision was made for the establishment of trade unions and works councils, but no district-level workers' councils and no industrial councils were ever formed.[33] Resistance in the private sector, together with disagreement within the SPD, meant that the workers' councils system as envisaged by the socialist-democratic government was never fully achieved.

I argue that the main reason behind the ineffectiveness of the workers' councils system under the Weimar Republic lies in the fallacies of the strategy of social reform. The Weimar state sought merely to ameliorate the imbalance and to contain the contradiction between labour and capital, through social reform, captured in the notion of 'economic democracy' and the project of 'constitutionalisation of labour relations'. The result was the deflation of the labour movement. Hugo Sinzheimer, as a professor of law and sociology, was responsible in large measure for the theorisation of German labour law. As parliamentary representative for the SPD, he was directly involved in drafting the Weimar constitution and labour statutes.[34] According to him, an imbalance of power between capital and labour ('property' and 'labour', as he called it) was *inherent* in the capitalist mode of production.[35] He thus proposed the adoption of an economic constitution, which was necessary to adjust

---

33 Ibid.
34 Ibid., 349–350.
35 Similar views were expressed by another major exponent of Weimar's social constitution of labour. Otto Kahn-Freund recognised the existence of a conflict, inherent to any advanced industrial society, between the aims of 'management' and those of 'labour', involving the matter of the distribution of the profits of an enterprise: management's priority is to maximise investment, and labour's is to maximize consumption; Ibid., 353.

this imbalance in favour of labour by enabling workers to participate in managerial decision-making on par with capital.[36]

However, the contradiction between Weimar's proclamations and the eventual failure to meet them is a historical fact. The question that Weimar and its supporters failed to ask is, 'what is the *root cause* for the imbalance of power between capital and labour?' This is the key to understanding how the balance might shift in favour of labour. What is the origin of inequality in bargaining power, if not the issue of ownership of the means of production? Capitalist relations of production are based on the subordinate position of labour with regards to capital. Capital as a social relation cannot be established and reproduced, unless on the basis of a fundamental contradiction between the private ownership of the means of production and the socialisation of the labour process.

Leaving the issue of ownership of the means of production untouched necessarily means that the main premise, upon which the capitalist exploitative relations are founded, is sustained and reproduced. If capitalist ownership of the means of production is taken for granted, then the conflict between capital and labour is ineradicable, and it is a matter of containing it and reproducing it. But, the reproduction of the capitalist system of contradictory relations eventually leads to the demise of the welfare-corporate form once it can no longer guarantee conditions of intensified exploitation. The reproduction of the fundamental capitalist premise means that generally—not only in interwar Germany but also in the post-war Western world—labour law and the welfare state form are allowed to exist so long as they serve this objective function of reproduction.

The Weimar form—and any other example of a bourgeois social-democratic regime—aims to right the injustices inherent in capitalism, but not in an absolute manner. It fails to address the core issues of production of wealth, relations of production and ownership of the means of production. It merely addresses inadequately the issue of distribution of wealth, exchange relations and negotiations.[37] Labour

---

36 Ibid., 345.
37 This occurs even though, arguably, labour legislation deals with the production process itself, by regulating, for instance, the limits to the working day and other conditions for the consumption of labour power. Nevertheless, the working day can be limited in case of capitalist policies that favour the extraction of relative surplus value with emphasis on technological innovation and reducing the socially necessary labour to produce a use-value, but this is not the case in a system based on absolute surplus value where the thirst for profit can only be satisfied by extending the working day and intensifying the exploitation of the labour force.

regulation presupposes both capitalist ownership and class division/exploitation while seeking to ameliorate their effects. The fundamental basis of the German capitalist social formation (i.e. private ownership) was preserved by the Weimar welfare state. Democratic input in decision-making did not contest with this, despite ameliorating some of its effects on labouring classes.

It has been argued that where Sinzheimer and his followers broke with Marx was in their belief that social justice and democracy could be achieved within the confines of the parliamentary system, through the extension of democracy from the political sphere to the economic sphere (i.e. through the constitutionalisation of industrial relations).[38] The social-democratic characteristics of the Weimar form are to a certain extent a manifestation of this particular tendency in the labour movement: a tendency that rejects the revolutionary road for a more evolutionary path of social reform through the introduction of 'socialist' policies in the bourgeois parliament; a tendency that survives until today in the Eurocommunist current.

Writing in a more recent context and arguing for an alternative to parliamentarism, István Mészáros warned against the corrosive effects caused by the full conformity of the various working class representatives to the 'rules of the parliamentary game'.[39] In particular, Mészáros quoted Rosa Luxembourg and her warning against the 'theoretical and political vacuity of the unfulfillable 'evolutionary' prescriptions': 'parliamentarism provides the soil for such illusions of current opportunism as overvaluation of social reforms, class and party collaboration, the hope of a pacific development towards socialism, etc'.[40] For Luxembourg—and Mészáros—parliamentarism aims at dissolving the class-conscious sector of the working class into the amorphous mass of the mythical 'electorate'. It can be argued that the result of parliamentarism in interwar Germany was the dissolution of the most active and class-conscious sector of the labour movement, which had compromised its freedom of action by reliance on state agencies to compensate for its lessened bargaining power. Therefore, in that context it was the life of the working-class movement that 'died out' because of its entrapment into reformist policies.

A comparison with the current predicament can only strengthen the argument for the need to revisit these abandoned debates that revolved

---

38 Dukes, *Constitutionalizing Employment Relations*, 347.
39 István Mészáros, *Historical Actuality of the Socialist Offensive* (London: Bookmarks Publications, 2010), 11.
40 Ibid., 14.

88 The Supersession of the bourgeois state

around the concept of dictatorship. After all, the Eurocommunist strategy influenced by Poulantzas's views was the intellectual offspring of the social-democratic strategy of the Second International. According to Ellen Meiksins Wood, Poulantzas's Eurocommunist analysis of the state is 'guilty' of the

> inverted instrumentalism which he had earlier rejected, the social-democratic notion that the state, or pieces of it, can pass, like an 'object coveted by the various classes', from the hands of the dominant class to those of the dominated, thereby effecting the transition from capitalism to socialism.[41]

In the aftermath of the most devastating and synchronised global capitalist crisis since the 1930s, the neoliberal onslaught against workers' rights and the worsening of the working and living conditions are proof of the precarious nature of concessions won by the working class within the confines of the capitalist state, as well as the failure of parliamentary institutions to lead the transition to socialism. The neoliberal turn of the old social-democratic parties since the 1980s throughout the Western world was accompanied by the social-democratisation and eventual marginalisation in the political spectrum of Eurocommunist parties. This process culminated in the social-democratic turn of Syriza, the last of the Eurocommunist parties that posed for a governing position in decades. Syriza ended up implementing neoliberal policies, despite being voted to power on the exact opposite mandate (i.e. to abolish these policies). Leaving aside the complexity of the (national and international) forces at play in the process of Syriza's transformation from a party based on Eurocommunist principles to a social-democratic party, I argue that this development has to be assessed as the last—albeit not necessarily final—step in a long process of Eurocommunist parties trading off the revolutionary characteristics of workers' parties for a place in the bourgeois system of distribution of power.

On this basis, I argue that it is essential to reopen the debate on the Marxist concept of dictatorship and re-evaluate the significant consequences of its theoretical rejection and political abandonment since the 1970s. This concept has significant analytical value to understanding what is common in the welfare state form and the neoliberal form—or the liberal democratic state and the authoritarian state form (i.e. the fact that all these forms reproduce the political rule of the bourgeoisie)—as well as to grasp what necessitates the change from one

---

41 Wood, *Retreat from Class*, 44.

state form to another. As we saw in the previous chapters, the reproduction of the political rule of the bourgeois class is ensured by a mixture of coercive and consensual, repressive and ideological measures, depending on the level of development of class struggle and the intensification of socio-economic contradictions. The factors that determine this change are best captured by the Marxist concept of dictatorship.

Dictatorship of the proletariat

The Marxist concept of dictatorship does not merely refer to the form of government. It is a wider concept. It refers to the totality of social relations that determine the class rule and the form of its exercise in a social formation. However, the term dictatorship was not used arbitrarily by Marx and the Marxist tradition. It signifies a transitional period to establish a new society. These are the themes that I explore in this section. In the first instance, I establish that the Marxist–Leninist definition of class dictatorship is wider than the formalist conception of dictatorship; then I proceed with the specific characteristics that the concept of dictatorship captures with regards to the process of socialist construction.

We begin with the view that the Marxist concept of dictatorship is not just about the form of government but about class rule. This is why its analysis cannot be carried out in the abstract, but always in concrete relation to the rule of a specific class: when we speak of the dictatorship of the bourgeoisie or the dictatorship of the proletariat, we have to consider the specific characteristics that distinguish the rule of one class from the rule of the other. For instance, to speak of the dictatorship of the bourgeoisie is to acknowledge that there exists a material threshold below which, even if the government is taken over by representatives of the workers, state power remains in the hands of the bourgeoisie, which will either make use of a 'socialist' government for its own ends (as in the case of the SPD in interwar Germany and Syriza in Greece), or overthrow it and crush the mass movement (as in the case of Allende in Chile).[42] This is, after all, what was established in the discussion of historical examples in the previous chapters (i.e. the use of dictatorial institutions and regimes to reproduce bourgeois rule).

So, the concept of dictatorship is necessary to explain the failure of 'pro-people' governments and the different methods of reproduction of the bourgeois state. This is precisely what Eurocommunist analyses

---

42 See Robert Barros, *Constitutionalism and Dictatorship: Pinochet, the Junta, and the 1980 Constitution* (Cambridge: Cambridge University Press, 2002).

lack, as they repeat the views of the Second International on the state and the proletarian strategy. The Eurocommunist critique of dictatorship follows the social-democratic critique carried out, most notably by Karl Kautsky, in the context of the Second International. This critique was made on the basis of an abstract opposition between democracy and dictatorship. It has been argued that this abstract opposition is steeped in bourgeois legal ideology, 'which reappears within the labour movement itself in the form of opportunism'.[43] The purpose of bourgeois legal ideology is to ensure the reproduction of social norms by presenting capitalist social relations as natural necessities. Legal ideology operates on a different plane than the law itself. It has to do not so much with sanctioning legal restraints, but with legitimising social relations, operating on the plane of consciousness. After all, visible chains can be broken but behaviours considered normal are harder to change. Bourgeois legal ideology ceaselessly explains that 'the law is its own source' and that the opposition between democracy (in the abstract) and dictatorship (in the abstract) is an absolute opposition.[44]

This means that grasping the difference between the formalist conception of democracy–dictatorship and the Marxist conception of these terms is essential for the process of emancipation. It also means that the process of emancipation is necessarily a long and arduous process of shifting deeply ingrained habits. Emancipation can only be the result of a conscious struggle to restructure and redefine every aspect of the social totality. Lenin's work on the concept of dictatorship is based on such a view. According to him, the dictatorship of the proletariat is a 'persistent struggle bloody and bloodless, violent and peaceful, military and economic, educational and administrative—against the forces and traditions of the old society'.[45] However, Lenin understood that the 'force of habit' is 'a most formidable force' that cannot change as long as the bourgeois state and the mechanisms that reproduce bourgeois ideology survive. He understands that the state rests on a relation of forces permeated by irreconcilable contradictions. Law cannot be the basis for this power. The dictatorship of the class stands above the law.

This is why, for both Marx and Lenin, the form of the proletarian state is established on a fundamental precondition (i.e. the suppression of the standing bourgeois army and the substitution of the armed people

---

43 Etienne Balibar, *On the Dictatorship of the Proletariat* (London: NLB, 1977), 67.
44 Ibid.
45 V.I. Lenin, '"Left-Wing" Communism: An Infantile Disorder', in *Collected Works: Volume 31* (Moscow: Progress Publishers, 1974), 44.

for it). This was the first decree of the Paris Commune. According to Marx, this decree was 'fact transformed into an institution'.[46] Paris, 'the social stronghold of the French working class', could resist 'the attempt of Thiers and the Rurals to restore and perpetuate that old governmental power bequeathed to them by the Empire' only because it had rid itself of the army and replaced it by a National Guard, the bulk of which consisted of working men.[47] The necessity of armed revolution that Marx and Engels concluded from the experience of the Paris Commune is expressed in the statement that 'the working class cannot simply lay hold of the ready-made State machinery, and wield it for its own purposes'.[48] It is safe to argue then that the revolutionary aspect is essential to the Marxist analysis of the state and so is the concept of dictatorship, which takes on the relationship between law and revolution.

I argue that the formalist opposition between democracy and dictatorship manifests and presupposes the rejection of the revolutionary elements of Marx's thought. Kautsky's accusations of a 'Bolshevik dictatorship', as well as Poulantzas's analysis of Soviet statism, interpret the Marxist view of dictatorship as a formalist conception that seeks to establish the rule of an 'enlightened minority'. On the contrary, I argue that these 'critiques' are themselves based on a formalist conception of democracy and dictatorship. The abstract antithesis between democracy and dictatorship is cancelled out, or rather superseded, in Lenin's exposition of the democratic form of government in the dictatorship of the proletariat. In his *The State and Revolution*, Lenin speaks of the form of the proletarian state as consisting of 'simple and self-evident democratic measures', such as the complete electivity of all officials without exception, their subjection to recall at any time, and the reduction of their salaries to the level of an ordinary 'workman's wages'.[49]

Nevertheless, these measures would '*acquire their full meaning and significance only in connection with the "expropriation of the expropriators*" being either accomplished or prepared, i.e. with the transition of capitalist ownership of the means of production into social ownership'.[50] Therefore, according to Lenin, the essence of class dictatorship is determined not so much from the issues of legality or illegality, violence or peacefulness of the path, but from the issue ownership of the

---

46 Karl Marx, 'The Civil War in France', in Karl Marx and Friedrich Engels, *Collected Works: Volume 22* (London: Lawrence and Wishart, 2010), 331.
47 Ibid.
48 Ibid., 328.
49 V.I. Lenin, *The State and Revolution* (London: Penguin Press, 2009), 40.
50 Ibid., emphasis added.

means of production. This point proves that the dialectical concept of dictatorship is a many-sided concept that refers to the totality of social relations. Ownership of the means of production, the existence of the law of value, or the gradual supersession of the latter by the law of balanced development of the economy, are factors that ultimately determine the nature of class dictatorship. The dictatorship of the proletariat may appear in a political form that is more democratic than the liberal democratic form of bourgeois dictatorship, but for this to happen a series of issues needs to be addressed: education, working conditions, living conditions and the elimination of social contradictions.

It is interesting here to look at the remarks made by one of history's most well-known 'dictators' on the prerequisites for a fuller democracy. Showing the depth of Marxist analysis, Stalin spoke of the 'necessity to ensure such a cultural advancement of society as will secure for all members of society the all-round development of their physical and mental abilities', for the members of society to 'be in a position to receive an education sufficient to enable them to be active agents of social development' and 'in a position freely to choose their occupations and not be tied all their lives, owing to the existing division of labour, to one occupation'.[51] This all-round development of physical and mental abilities is a prerequisite for a full democracy, or rather for the association of free producers that Marx defined as communist society. Moreover, it can only be the result of a long and arduous process of struggle and social restructuring that affects every aspect of living and working conditions and social relations. According to Stalin, to achieve this,

> it is necessary, first of all, to shorten the working day at least to six, and subsequently to five hours. This is needed in order that the members of society might have the necessary free time to receive an all-round education. It is necessary, further, to introduce universal compulsory polytechnical education, which is required in order that the members of society might be able freely to choose their occupations and not be tied to one occupation all their lives. It is likewise necessary that housing conditions should be radically improved, and that real wages of workers and employees should be at least doubled, if not more, both by means of direct increases of wages and salaries, and, more especially, by further systematic reductions of prices for consumer goods.[52]

---

51 Joseph Stalin, *Economic Problems of Socialism in the USSR* (Peking: Foreign Language Press, 1972), 70.
52 Ibid.

The all-round development of the individual in the process of socialist construction becomes a prerequisite for the development of the political form of the proletarian state and its eventual abolition in communist society. As Evald Ilyenkov put it,

> the question of building a communist society amounts to the converting of each individual from a one sided professional—from a slave of the division of labour system—into an all-around personality, a real master (proprietor) of the material and spiritual culture created by all mankind.[53]

I argue that the above passage shifts the focus from a formalist discussion of democracy and dictatorship to a many-sided understanding of the interwoven processes of political formation and socio-economic change. The democratic form of the dictatorship of the proletariat is a unity of form and content; it combines the processes of political organisation of the working class and the popular strata with the organisation of production and the restructuring of the general material conditions.

Furthermore, the concept of dictatorship of the proletariat cannot be grasped unless we understand it as a historical period of transition and development of the conditions for the elimination of classes, as well as the abolition of class rule and the state. This process, which in Marxist discourse is known as the process of the 'withering away' of the state—and law—is crucial for understanding what dictatorship of the proletariat stands for. The rule of the proletariat, exercised through the proletarian state, is only reproduced to lead to the elimination of class rule altogether. It can be argued that this element of transitionality to a new classless society, without the need for repression and enforceable rules, is precisely what lends this historical epoch the characterisation of dictatorship.

The dictatorship of the proletariat lasts as long as the state withers away. These two terms indicate both the gradual and the spontaneous nature of the process. For Lenin, the question of the withering away of the state is a question of habit and the development of the necessary economic conditions for such habits to develop. Lenin observes 'millions of occasions' where people readily become 'accustomed to observing the necessary rules of social intercourse when there is no exploitation, when there is nothing that arouses indignation, evokes

---

53 E.V. Ilyenkov, 'From the Marxist-Leninist Point of View', in Nicholas Lobkowicz (ed.), *Marx and the Western World* (London: University of Notre Dame Press, 1967), 391–407.

protest and revolt, and creates the need for suppression'.[54] This process of political transformation—more accurately the process of abolition of the political—is linked to the development of productive forces and relations.

The economic basis for this habit to take over involves such a high development of communist production that the distribution of products will not call for a system of norms to regulate how many products are to be received by each; each will take freely 'according to their needs'.[55] Additionally, individuals will have become 'so accustomed to observing the fundamental rules of social intercourse', when their labour is so productive, 'that they will voluntarily work "according to their ability"'.[56] Communist society, based on the productive and distributive principle 'from each according to their ability, to each according to their needs', will be the result of a process of struggle for eliminating the contradictions of capitalist society. These contradictions include not just class divisions, or the contradiction between the private ownership of the means of production and the socialised labour process, but also the contradictions between mental and physical labour, town and country, etc. Marx defines as 'revolutionary dictatorship of the proletariat' the period of political transition between capitalist and communist society.[57] This period of transition corresponds to the first stage of communist society 'not as it has *developed* on its own foundations, but, on the contrary, just as it *emerges* from capitalist society'; still stamped with the 'birthmarks' of the capitalist society.[58] These 'birthmarks' signify the contradictions that this first phase of the communist society inherits from capitalism, including the contradiction between town and country, manual and intellectual labour, commodity and socialist production.

These 'birthmarks' necessitate the existence of law and the state during this first phase of immature communism. Law does not wither away in the dictatorship of the proletariat. It still has a role to play in the process of socialist construction. In fact, the defects of the first phase of communist society are bound to be reflected in the proletarian state and legal form. Marx argued that 'right can never be higher than the economic structure of society and its cultural development conditioned thereby'.[59] Lenin furthered this point by claiming that 'this first phase

---

54 Lenin, *The State and Revolution*, 80.
55 Ibid., 87.
56 Ibid., 86.
57 Karl Marx, 'Critique of the Gotha Programme', in Karl Marx and Friedrich Engels, *Collected Works: Volume 24* (London: Lawrence and Wishart, 2010), 95.
58 Ibid., 85, emphasis in original.
59 Ibid., 87.

The Supersession of the bourgeois state 95

of communism cannot yet provide justice and equality, as differences, and unjust differences, in wealth still persist'.[60] The reason for these 'unjust differences' is the persistence of the distributive principle 'to each according to his labour'. The principle according to which 'a given amount of labour in one form is exchanged for an equal amount of labour in another form' applies in socialism (i.e. immature communism) with regards to the distribution of individual means of consumption.[61]

The 'injustice', which consists in the distribution of consumer goods 'according to the amount of labour performed'—and not according to needs—remains in the first phase. However, the 'injustice' of the individual ownership of the means of production is abolished. Consequently, the exploitation of man by man becomes impossible, and this is the first major step to emancipation. Following this line of thought, it has been argued that socialist-proletarian law corresponds already to a different socio-economic content and cannot be reduced to bourgeois law.[62] In the context of the Soviet Union, it was argued

---

60 Lenin, *The State and Revolution* (2009), 84.
61 Marx, *Critique of the Gotha Programme*, 86.
62 There was intense debate among legal and political theorists around the question of socialist law during the first decade of existence of the Soviet Union. Evgeny Pashukanis, perhaps the most well-known Soviet legal theorist, in his 1924 'General Theory of Law and Marxism' argued that commodity exchange is the reason for the existence of law. The legal subject, on whom the entire legal order is built, first appears in the exchange transaction; see Evgeny Pashukanis, *Selected Writings on Marxism and Law* (London: Academic Press, 1980), 79. Therefore, according to Pashukanis, the abolition of commodity exchange should lead immediately to the abolition of law. Such a thing as 'socialist law' cannot exist as it is a contradiction in terms. On the contrary, other writers opposed this view and criticised Pashukanis's theory of the commodity form, holding that soviet law is radically different from bourgeois law, despite the formal resemblance. For Andrey Vyshinsky, Soviet law cannot be reduced to bourgeois law. It rather corresponds to a different socio-economic content, and, as a result, it assumes a partially different form. Soviet law is characterized by 'the tendency to reduce the role of coercion, the tendency to increase the participation of all people in the running of the state, the tendency to transfer state functions to social organization, the tendency of the state to gradually drop its political character'; see Rett R. Ludwikowski, 'Socialist Legal Theory in the Post-Pashukanis Era', 10 *Boston College International & Comparative Law Review*, 323, 325. It is interesting to note that Pashukanis himself in his later works criticised his earlier analyses and recognised the methodological error of putting emphasis solely on the limited aspect of exchange relations, while ignoring the other aspects of the totality of relations of production. So, by 1936 Pashukanis had criticised his 'General Theory', where 'law, state and morality were simply declared to be bourgeois forms which cannot be filled with socialist content'; see Evgeny Pashukanis, 'State and Law under Socialism', partially translated into English in Michael Jaworskyj (ed.), *Soviet Political Thought: An Anthology* (Johns Hopkins University Press, 1967), 315–323.

that Soviet law is different from bourgeois law in that it recognises no class differences, because everyone is a worker like everyone else. But in 'tacitly recognising unequal individual endowment, and thus productive capacity as natural privilege', 'equal right in socialism is still unequal right for unequal labour'.[63]

The 'narrow horizon of bourgeois right' is not yet crossed in its entirety as long as social contradictions remain. The emancipatory process does not stop with the crushing of the bourgeois state and the overtaking of state power by the working class and its allies. Therefore, the role of law in this process extends to the process of socialist construction and the period of the dictatorship of the proletariat. If the goal of the emancipatory process is the 'realm of freedom' (i.e. communism) the long and arduous process to establish the conditions for a communist society involves a historical period when law still exists, albeit corresponding to a different socio-economic content and, consequently, assuming a partially different form. Law still operates in the context of a social formation where class contradictions may have been eliminated, but some contradictions remain (such as the ones between manual and intellectual labour, skilled and unskilled labour, town and country), and some of them may be antagonistic in nature (such as the one between commodity and socialist production). The nature of contradictions in socialism was widely debated, not only among economists, but also among philosophers and legal theorists.[64]

The concept of the dictatorship of the proletariat was central in the discussion of the remaining contradictions, the inherited 'defects', in Soviet society. According to Thomas Weston,[65] historian of soviet philosophy, the notion of 'non-antagonistic contradictions' was introduced by Soviet philosophers in the early 1930s. The fundamental claim of the relevant analyses was that 'non-antagonistic contradictions' were resolved through a gradual process of merging or equating of opposites, and not through the intensification of the struggle and radical transformation. Other formulations described the resolution of a 'non-antagonistic contradiction' gradually, without a radical outburst, without the need of violence or the destruction of one of the sides of the contradiction.

This notion was used extensively in Soviet philosophical, political and economic works. On the one hand, some writers recognised the

---

63 Marx, *Critique of the Gotha Programme*, 87.
64 See footnote 62.
65 Thomas Weston, 'The Concept of Non-Antagonistic Contradictions in Soviet Philosophy', 72 *Science and Society*, 427–428.

existence of contradictions in Soviet society, but denied that these may develop in an antagonistic manner. According to Pavel Yudin, there were no antagonistic contradictions bearing on Soviet society and there were no social groups or forces 'opposed to the construction of communism or attached to the old'.[66] On the other hand, fewer theorists, with Evald Ilyenkov as the most prominent among them, openly argued for a clear demarcation between the contradictory spheres of market relations and socialist production, which co-existed in Soviet society.[67] For Ilyenkov, the contradiction between the capitalist law of value and the socialist law of balanced development was potentially antagonistic. Therefore, he stressed the need to carry on with the revolutionary struggle of the working class, in conditions of socialist construction, until the elimination of all social contradictions.[68]

If we accept that the contradiction between commodity production and socialist production existed and was in fact an antagonistic (or at least potentially antagonistic) contradiction in Soviet society, then it can be argued that the 1965 reforms, known as the Koshigin reforms, which strengthened the market elements of Soviet relations of production, were due to undervaluation of the antagonistic nature of these contradictions. The historical experience of socialist regimes showed that the process of socialist construction contains the possibility of a reversal and a retreat towards capitalism. The contradictions of Soviet society proved to be antagonistic, and the social resistance (by kolkhoz peasants as well as executives in agricultural production and industry) to the process of expansion and deepening of the socialist relations of production was expressed, at an ideological and political level, through struggle internal to the Communist Party of the Soviet Union (CPSU) that began in the early 1950s. This struggle resulted in the victory of the right opportunist deviation, as evidenced in the decisions adopted in the 20th Congress of the CPSU and the theoretical acceptance of the law of value as a law of socialism. The practical adoption of political choices that expanded commodity production, in the name of correcting weaknesses in Central Planning and in the administration of

---

66 Pavel Yudin, *From Socialism to Communism* (Moscow: Progress Publishers, 1963), 11.
67 For an overview of the debate on the operation of the law of value in socialist production and its relationship to the socialist law of balanced development, see Stalin, *Economic Problems in the USSR*, 18–23.
68 E.V. Ilyenkov, 'Letter to Yu. A. Zhdanov 18.01.1968', in *Personality and Creativity* (in Russian) (Moscow: Jazyki russkoj kul'tury, 1999), 258–261.

the socialist productive units, confirmed the antagonistic nature of the contradiction between market relations and socialist production.[69]

These contradictions were also reflected in the field of public law. The concept of 'non-antagonistic contradictions' seems to have influenced the drafting of the 1936 Soviet Constitution. In his report on the Draft Constitution, Stalin emphasised that, 'unlike bourgeois constitutions, the draft of the new Constitution of the U.S.S.R. proceeds from the fact that there are no longer any antagonistic classes in society'.[70] However, he did not consider the new Constitution as abandoning the strategy of the dictatorship of the proletariat. Instead he saw it as 'the broadening of the basis of the dictatorship of the working class and the transformation of the dictatorship into a more flexible, and, consequently, a more powerful system of guidance of society by the state'.[71] Nevertheless, the undervaluation of the potentially antagonistic nature of contradictions in the process of socialist construction was arguably reflected in the adoption of the new electoral principle (i.e. universal direct suffrage on the basis of geographic constituencies[72]) instead of indirect election of the members of the All-Russian Congress of Soviets from the local soviets.

The argument can be made that the downgrading of the role of production units as nuclei of political organisations had a negative impact on the class composition of the higher state organs and on the application of the right of recall of delegates. In this way, the Soviet constitutional law might have played a role in enhancing counter-revolutionary tendencies, even unintentionally. However, this claim needs to be studied and researched further. What is instead undeniable is the influence that the intra-party struggle and the victory of the right opportunist forces had on the abolition of the principle of the dictatorship of the proletariat after the 20th Congress of the CPSU. The view was established in the 1961 Programme of the CPSU that the 'dictatorship of the proletariat had fulfilled its historic mission and has ceased to be indispensable in the USSR'.[73] The reason for this was the conclusion of the first

---

69 See Abraham Katz, *The Politics of Economic Reform*, (New York: Praeger Publishers, 1972).
70 Joseph Stalin, 'On the Draft Constitution of the U.S.S.R.', in Joseph Stalin, *Works: Volume 14*, (London: Red Star Press Ltd., 1978), 167.
71 Stalin, *Economic Problems in the USSR*, 177.
72 Article 34 of the Constitution provided that 'the Soviet of the Union is elected by the citizens of the U.S.S.R. according to electoral areas on the basis of one deputy for every 300,000 of the population'.
73 See *Programme of the Communist Party of the Soviet Union* (Moscow: Foreign Languages Publishing House, 1961).

phase of communism and the victory of socialism. This meant that the state, which initially 'arose as a state of the dictatorship of the proletariat', in this new stage became 'a state of the entire people, an organ expressing the interests and will of the people as a whole'.[74]

It is obvious that this conclusion relies on the unconditional acceptance of the view that there were no antagonistic contradictions in Soviet society, which could potentially reverse the process of socialist construction and initiate a retreat to capitalism. History proved otherwise. Thus, it can be argued that the view that the dictatorship of the proletariat had ceased to be necessary before the state withered away and could be replaced by a 'state of the entire people' might have contributed to the undervaluation of these contradictions that eventually proved antagonistic and gradually carried forward the process of counter-revolution.

To conclude, I argue that the concept of dictatorship of the proletariat is crucial to grasp that the social revolution is a process not restricted to the conquest of power. It rather includes the development of socialism and the elimination of the remaining contradictions, the 'defects' inherited from capitalist society. During the transitional period of the 'dictatorship of the proletariat' the class struggle of the working class continues, under new conditions, with other forms and means. Dictatorship of the proletariat signifies an ongoing battle for the abolition of every form of group and individual ownership over the means and products of production, the elimination of exploitation, as well as the abolition of every remaining contradiction (such as between mental and physical labour, town and country, etc.). These processes will eventually lead to the development of the communist consciousness, which corresponds to the directly social character of labour and enables the legal and state form and institutions to wither away. Consequently, from a Marxist standpoint, the dictatorship of the proletariat is necessary not only for the consolidation of the workers' state, but also during the process of socialist construction and until its maturation into the higher, communist stage (i.e. until the state and law wither away).

The Marxist concept of dictatorship proves to be different from the bourgeois formalist conceptions of the term. It refers not just to a republican institution or a type of regime (i.e. to the juridico-political form necessary to reproduce class rule in a situation of crisis) but to class rule itself. The class concept of dictatorship has a different content depending on the class whose rule it designates. There is no dictatorship in the abstract, but a dictatorship of the bourgeoisie or a dictatorship of

74 Ibid., 91.

the proletariat. The former refers to the rule of the bourgeoisie, which may appear in a variety of forms—from the form of the liberal democratic state to all kinds of dictatorial forms (military dictatorship, state of siege, fascist state, etc.) depending on the level of capitalist development and the intensification of socio-political contradictions. The latter refers to a historical epoch that is characterised by the rule of the working class and the process of building the (material and ideological) conditions for the abolition of socio-economic contradictions together with the juridico-political form. The Marxist concept of dictatorship refers, thus, to the unity of the socio-economic processes and the juridico-political form (i.e. the social totality). Contrary to accusations, it does not pay a blind eye to the juridico-political form. It places the issue of form in a central place but examines it together with the conditions that determine its appearance and disappearance.

5 Contribution to the theory of dictatorship

The concept of dictatorship signifies a process through which the state adjusts its form to reproduce itself, as well as the rule of the dominant social class. The dictatorial form is a form of exercise of public power, a specific mode of bourgeois class rule, whereby the state relies predominantly on repressive means to ensure the reproduction of the regime of power, property and production relations. The concept of dictatorship has three possible meanings. First, it can refer to the republican institution of dictatorship. This meaning originates in the classical Roman institution of *dictatura* and is now an essential aspect of the liberal-democratic state, enshrined in constitutional texts globally as the provision of a state of exception, martial law or state of emergency. The second meaning is wider and refers to the exceptional state form as a whole. It describes a specific type of regime that relies predominantly on repression and functions to reproduce class rule through a thorough reorganisation of the mode of exercise of state power, which involves the exercise of law-making powers. Historical examples such as Louis Bonaparte's regime, military dictatorships around the world, or fascist states would fall under this concept of dictatorship. The first two possible meanings of dictatorship both refer to *forms* of exercise of class rule and from now on will be jointly referred to as 'dictatorial form'. So, by dictatorial form we mean both the institution of dictatorship and the dictatorial type of regime. Last but not least, dictatorship can be used to signify class rule in general and not just one of the forms of its exercise.

As a concept relevant to the capitalist state form, dictatorship has historically played a part in political developments in the different epochs of capitalism. The particular characteristics of the dictatorial form are determined by the level of capitalist development and class struggle. There is no super-historical meaning of the concept. Instead I argue that the specific forms of dictatorship have to be studied in their historical context, as determined by the specific conjuncture of class struggle and capitalist development. For instance, the progressive role of the bourgeoisie and the process of radicalisation during the French Revolution, as well as the role of the state in the rise of the bourgeois class to dominance, have to be considered to understand why the Constituent Assembly and the Committee of Public Safety were characterised as dictatorial by the moderates. Similarly, the counter-revolutionary turn of the bourgeoisie by 1848 can account for the central role played by the dictatorial form during the period of the first uprisings of the proletariat, through the use of the 'state of siege' and the establishment of the Bonapartist regime. Last but not least, the state's interventionist role in the epoch of imperialism has to be taken into account to understand the process that gave rise to the fascist states in the interwar period.

Throughout these stages of development, the dictatorial form exhibits certain essential characteristics. These include the predominant role of repression, an element of temporariness and transitionality and a complex relationship with the law. The last two aspects of the dictatorial form are where the contradictions of this form are at their most evident. I argue that the irresolvable nature of these contradictions necessitates an understanding of dictatorship not simply as a form of exercise of class rule, but as unity of the different forms of class rule and class rule itself. I now examine the contradictions of the dictatorial form under the lens of the formalist conception of dictatorship (i.e. the conception that focuses solely on the juridico-political form and pays no attention to the issue of class power).

Schmitt's theory of dictatorship is the best example of a formalist conception of the term. As we saw in the first chapter, Schmitt distinguishes between two types of dictatorship, a 'commissarial' and a 'sovereign' type. The commissarial dictator acts on a strict and temporally limited mandate to safeguard the existing order, whereas the sovereign dictator exercises unlimited power to establish a new order. The equivocation between these two types and the contradictions of Schmitt's formalist theory of dictatorship unravel if we ask a simple question, such as: is a military dictatorship a sovereign or a commissarial dictatorship? The answer to this question, within the confines of the Schmittian discourse, would depend on the scope of powers conferred upon the dictatorial institutions. Are these only allowed executive decision-making or are they allowed to alter the law, even its highest form? The former type would be commissarial whereas the latter would be sovereign. This distinction already implies a separation—which is not so clear-cut—between generation and application of rules. Furthermore, it is important to consider the source of authority of this or the other kind of dictatorship.

Accordingly, a military dictatorship might be more accurately defined as a sovereign dictatorship because it generally entails altering the constitution and enacting general legislation (even though the characteristics of specific military dictatorships have to be examined on an ad hoc basis). However, if a military dictatorship is a type of sovereign dictatorship, who is the sovereign in such a case? Is it the army in the name of the people? For Schmitt, in the context of the French Revolution, sovereign is the National Convention in the name of the people. But does this 'in the name of' indicate the existence of a commissarial relationship? Are all types of dictatorship commissarial or does 'commissarial dictatorship' only capture the historical cases of states of siege, states of emergency, martial law, etc.? Sovereign and commissarial dictatorship seem to be in an equivocal relationship as they both appear to rely on a mandate to promote the 'salus populi': the former by protecting the existing order, and the latter by introducing a new one, both in the name of the people.

Another contradiction is apparent with regards to the traits of temporariness and transitionality. As we saw in the first chapter, Schmitt cites Bodin, according to whom permanence is a trait of sovereignty whereas temporariness is the essential element of dictatorship. The Decemviri were given as an example of sovereign—because of the mandate to create a new constitution—dictatorship—because their mandate was temporally limited. However, if dictatorship is always transitional and the sovereign dictator has an unlimited mandate, who is to decide when a sovereign dictatorship ends and when it gives its place to the new normality? If the measures required to ensure the reproduction of a regime under threat necessitate a degree of permanence, then permanence also becomes a trait of dictatorship. Nevertheless, permanence does not become an essential feature of Schmitt's concept of dictatorship, even though this contradiction eventually appears in Schmitt's famous definition of sovereignty. His definition ('sovereign is he who decides on the exception'[1]) reveals the equivocation between sovereignty and dictatorship by recognising the dictatorial decision as the locus of sovereignty.

Temporariness and permanence thus become relative to the mandate given to the dictator and to the nature of the measures necessary to protect the existing order or establish the new one. This is where a final contradiction reveals itself. If the law-generating function is the feature that distinguishes commissarial from sovereign dictatorship, then the transition from commissarial to sovereign dictatorship is inescapable.

1 Schmitt, *Political Theology*, 5.

Schmitt himself recognises this in his *Guardian of the Constitution*. In the imperialist phase of capitalism, the 'particular socio-economic situation' that the executive must address 'necessarily calls for activity that is substantially beyond commissarial action' and requires a 'structural historical transformation on a macroeconomic, social, and political scale' that can only be met by 'the constitution amending of sovereign dictatorship'.[2] As evidenced in the case of the establishment of the Nazi regime, the reproduction of conditions of capitalist production and the reproduction of bourgeois rule necessitate a transition from one type of dictatorship to the other.

I argue that these contradictions are due to the common function of the different dictatorial forms in reproducing the state power of the ruling class. Both the restoration of order and the establishment of a new order—in other words, both the restoration of normality and the establishment of a new normality—betray a common necessity: the necessity to restore capitalist normality through whatever means necessary. What is more, this necessity underlies both exceptional and normal forms of exercise of public power. This necessity unites normal and exceptional forms as evidenced in the succession of juridico-political forms in Germany during the interwar period. The normality of the Weimar Republic was replaced by the exceptional normality of the Nazi state, once the former could not accommodate the contradictions it was initially set up to reproduce. The dictatorial form, as well as the normal bourgeois juridico-political form, ultimately functions to guarantee the uninterrupted continuity of bourgeois rule and capitalist production. They are different forms, but it is impossible to distinguish in an absolute manner one from the other, despite the best of efforts carried out by bourgeois theorists. This conclusion necessitates a re-evaluation of the concept of class dictatorship.

For a comprehensive understanding of dictatorship, it is essential to examine the concrete socio-economic processes that necessitate the assumption of the dictatorial form. These can be broadly classified as the class and intra-class contradictions that are intensified in a situation of crisis, consequently threatening the reproduction of capitalist social relations. In the second and third chapters, the concept of hegemony was used to describe the complex nature of such situations. Hegemony is different from rule. Hegemony implies a relation of leadership, where the leader and the followers are on the same side and heading towards the same direction. Contrariwise, rule implies that the ruler and the ruled may stand opposed to each other. This is a difference that

---

2 McCormick, *From Constitutional Technique to Caesarist Ploy*, 207.

captures the nuance of the mechanism of consent as opposed to force and command. I argue that hegemony is part of the process of class dictatorship. Dictatorship in the Marxist sense of the term includes both repression and ideology (i.e. both mechanisms for the generation and organisation of consent and mechanisms of repression). In that sense hegemony is a mode of class rule, a category of class rule. The process of securing the consent of the exploited and oppressed is part of the process of exercising class rule. The dominant class may rule as well as lead—although they can only truly lead the members of their own class because of the irreducible contradiction that separates them from the dominated classes. It may reproduce its rule and its hegemonic position through repressive and ideological means.

During periods of normality, the reproduction of class rule is carried out predominantly on the basis of ideological means and consensus-generating mechanisms—even though the accuracy of this statement itself depends on the level of capitalist development and the specific conjuncture of class struggle in the 'normal' period considered. Hegemony is sustained through ideological apparatuses that carefully articulate and blur the lines between immediate and strategic interests of different classes. These ideological mechanisms sustain social reproduction by affecting processes of class consciousness. The narrow economic interests of the ruling class are presented as general and universal to attract multiple groups. These ideological mechanisms have a material basis, not only in the sense of concessions to the dominated classes but also in the sense of them being ingrained in social, cultural and moral practices and rituals.

Historically, situations of crisis and intensified socio-economic contradictions result in a difficulty on behalf of the ruling class to generate mechanisms of legitimation. Of course, the exact extent of this difficulty depends on the concrete socio-economic conditions. For instance, in the nineteenth century a mild economic crisis could have severe implications for the reproduction of bourgeois rule, because the bourgeoisie was still in the process of consolidating its rule. As we saw in the second chapter, by 1848 the weapons that the bourgeoisie had used against the old feudal order had been turned against it by the toiling classes. As a result, 'even bourgeois liberalism [was] declared socialistic'[3] and the liberal state gave its place to the Bonapartist dictatorship. On the contrary, a much more acute capitalist crisis in the twenty-first century did not give rise to any kind of dictatorial state form *tout court*. In the twenty-first century the specific conjuncture of class struggle is such

---

3 Karl Marx, *The Eighteenth Brumaire of Louis Bonaparte*, 141.

that it allows the bourgeois class to reproduce its rule predominantly on the basis of ideologico-political means (such as the dissemination of the principles of 'there is no alternative' and lesser-evilism). Yet, still in this context, processes of increasing authoritarianism are proliferating.

The crisis of hegemony is accompanied by deep political and institutional crisis. Symptoms include a crisis of party representation that leads to the radicalisation of factions of the ruling class towards exceptional state forms, such as military dictatorship, a proliferation of bourgeois organisations that tend to address this crisis in party representation, and a crisis in the dominant ideology. Restoring order through limited use of force or suspension of rights is not enough, if such a crisis has occurred. Rather, a complete reorganisation of the state apparatuses is necessary. This reorganisation involves a different combination of the modes of class rule (i.e. of repression as the mode of class rule enforced by violence and ideology as the mode secured by consent), which results in the dictatorial form. It also involves a rebalancing of forces between the different state apparatuses and a displacement of the dominant branch of apparatus. Most commonly, the dominant position will belong to a branch of the repressive state apparatus (i.e. the army in a military dictatorship, civil administration in the Bonapartist state or the political police in the fascist state), but ideological state apparatuses (such as the party or the Church) can also occupy the dominant position in the new configuration of power.

What these dictatorial forms have in common, however, is the devaluation of the bourgeois parliament, as well as the suspension of the electoral principle. This suspension has far-reaching consequences and affects all state apparatuses, as well as it gives rise to new concepts and principles of public law and political decision-making. As far as the relationship between the ruling class and the dominated classes is concerned, the electoral system is a means of ideological indoctrination of the latter. Its suspension is a feature of the failure of the normal parliamentary form to carry out this indoctrination, most probably due to the crisis of legitimacy of the mainstream political parties in a situation of crisis. As far as the relationship between different factions of the ruling class is concerned, elections are a form of political organisation of the alliance that ensures the circulation of power within the power bloc. The suspension of the electoral principle affects both the class and the intra-class relations and contradictions and gives rise to new forms and new problems regarding these.

For instance, the suspension of the parliamentary elections in Nazi Germany gave rise to a plebiscitarian form of legitimacy, embodied in the principles of 'leadership' and 'ethnic identity'. As we saw in the third chapter, plebiscitarianism provided the legitimating mechanism necessary for the conditions of intensified exploitation. For this reason, the effect of the leadership principle was not limited to constitutional law but covered areas of economic policy and operated in the field of labour relations. The 'Law for the Organization of National Labour' of 1934 set up the German Labour Front as the inclusive organization of German manual and intellectual workers, who were no longer called by the old names but were referred to as 'leaders' and 'followers'. One of the effects of the operation of the leadership principle was that the interests of workers (i.e. the followers) were presented as identical to the interests of capitalists (i.e. the leaders).

In the context of Nazi Germany, the principles of leadership and ethnic identity also functioned to secure the unity of the ruling class against centrifugal tendencies. However, the reorganisation of class rule modalities and the shift of the balance of forces between the different state apparatuses in the dictatorial form mean that intra-class contradictions have to be filtered through new avenues. The problem arises from the absence of the mediating flexibilities of the republican form. These are essential for the mediation of intra-class contradictions but they are absent in the dictatorial form. This callousness of the dictatorial form means that the balance of forces cannot anymore change with a minimum amount of upheaval in the state apparatus because dictatorial regimes are incapable of reforming themselves.

This is a key point for the discussion of what replaces the dictatorial form. This discussion is related to another point developed in the previous chapters (i.e. the relative autonomy dialectics). We examined Engels's statement about Bonapartism being the 'true religion' of the bourgeoisie and understood this to mean that Bonapartist dictatorship, based on the recruitment of the state apparatus from the petty bourgeois strata, provided a model for the operation of the bourgeois state and its class function. We discussed Poulantzas's view on this issue that the class origin of the individuals comprising the state apparatus does not determine the class nature of the state. The opposite is the case: a state whose members are not recruited from the ruling class may even more effectively carry out its class function under certain circumstances. The dictatorial form enhances the relative autonomy of the state and thus contributes to a more effective exercise of class rule as it obfuscates the class nature of the state under the guise of arbitrariness or irrationality. This sense of enhancement of the relative autonomy is also attributed to the lack of absolute coincidence of the policies pursued by the dictatorial state with the interests of the ruling class—even though this discrepancy can also be observed in the bourgeois republican form.

On the contrary, the abolition of representative institutions is certainly a factor that contributes to the reduction of the state's relative autonomy, as the destruction of political parties makes it harder for intra-class antagonisms, but also for class antagonisms, to be mediated. Furthermore, the open pursuit of class policies of intensified exploitation arguably makes it easier to expose the class nature of the dictatorial state. Therefore, there is a certain dialectics of enhancing and reducing the relative autonomy of the state in the dictatorial form.

All the aforementioned factors that condition the establishment of a dictatorial form in the epoch of imperialism necessitate the re-evaluation of the concept of 'class dictatorship'. The Marxist concept of dictatorship as class rule places emphasis on the class content of state power as the determining factor of the juridico-political form. The ruling class reproduces its dominant position through a combination of modes: coercion and consent, repression and ideology. The concept of class dictatorship sets this as the initial parameter for the examination of the dictatorial form, as well as all other forms of the bourgeois state. On this basis, it is essential to establish that the analytical value of the concept is to be found in the specificity of its class content. In other words, there is no class dictatorship in the abstract, but only dictatorship of the bourgeoisie and dictatorship of the proletariat. The reason why these two classes are the only classes that can rule in a specific social formation is to be found in Marx's analysis of the irreconcilable contradiction between these two classes.

The main class division in a capitalist social formation is the division between the capitalist class and the working class, because the private ownership of the means of production by the capitalist and the separation of the individual producer from the means of production (i.e. the property of the capitalist and the propertylessness of the proletariat) are the fundamental preconditions of the capitalist mode of production. The dictatorship of the bourgeoisie ultimately relies on the private ownership of the means of production by the capitalist class. This is the fundamental social relation that the bourgeois state reproduces in all its forms. Contrariwise, the dictatorship of the proletariat ultimately relies on and safeguards the social ownership of the means of production and actively participates in the struggle for the elimination of the socio-economic contradictions that socialist society inherits from capitalism.

Consequently, the qualitative difference between the two kinds of class dictatorship is located in their different aims and principles. The dictatorship of the bourgeoisie aims to reproduce bourgeois class rule, as well as the conditions of exploitation of labour power that enable capitalist profit. Under this prism, the dictatorial form is an essential element of the dictatorship of the bourgeoisie and its capacity to reproduce itself in the face of an existential threat. On the contrary, the dictatorship of the proletariat aims initially at the establishment, consolidation and reproduction of proletarian rule, but simultaneously it prioritises the abolition of conditions of exploitation as well as the abolition of all remaining social contradictions. The dictatorship of the proletariat reproduces the proletarian state and rule only to lead to the abolition of all forms of repression or domination. These principled aims set one class dictatorship wide apart from the other.

The concept of the dictatorship of the bourgeoisie denotes that even the most dictatorial state is not devoid of law and even the most liberal state contains the latent possibility of dictatorship. An element of arbitrariness may be necessary to reorganise the balance of forces between the dominant branches of the state, but legal certainty is also necessary to ensure the normality of capitalist production. Furthermore, every liberal state contains what Schmitt called the 'ever-present possibility of conflict'. The liberal form of the bourgeois state may allow for certain liberties and concessions to the dominated classes, but these find their absolute limit on the dominant component of the correlation of forces in capitalist society. As long as the reproduction of the conditions of capitalist production—and consequently of bourgeois rule—is threatened, the state may assume a dictatorial form to deal with this threat.

We arrive at the conclusion that the concept of class dictatorship refers to juridico-political processes in their unity with socio-economic processes. Rather than reducing form to content, the Marxist concept of dictatorship places emphasis on the form. One form of bourgeois government may be more democratic; in another form of bourgeois government, authoritarian elements might be more dominant. But if they both reproduce the fundamental condition of capitalist relations, can we not speak of two different forms of the bourgeois state (i.e. two different forms of bourgeois dictatorship)? I argue that this is not reductionism. The starting point is the difference between the two forms. But as much attention is paid to the form of decision-making (whether it is democratic or authoritarian), equal emphasis has to be put on the socio-economic relations reproduced by this form.

This method of analysis and the insights it provides into the workings of the bourgeois state are essential to understand the current predicament and the contemporary transformations of the state in the face of crisis. These transformations, in particular the juridico-political context within which the last capitalist crisis erupted and the forms the development of which it led to, have to be understood on the basis of the continuity between normal and exceptional forms in reproducing the conditions of capitalist production.

To understand why the most devastating capitalist crisis since the 1930s did not lead to the establishment of fascist dictatorships as it did during the interwar period, but only led to the development of authoritarian processes within the context of the liberal-democratic form, we have to consider the characteristics of the present phase of imperialism and the conjuncture of class struggle that this determines. A comprehensive study of imperialism falls outside the scope of our analysis but a few remarks on the current conjuncture of social forces are necessary to highlight the factors that ultimately determine the development of contemporary state form.

An initial factor that has to be taken into account is the context of counter-revolution and regression of the working-class movement that has characterised the last thirty years. The capitalist offensive on the working class was intensified throughout the world in the aftermath of the victory of the counter-revolution in the U.S.S.R. and the fall of the Soviet bloc. These developments together with the deleterious effect of the Eurocommunist tradition and political opportunism in the political organisations of the working class were among the factors that prepared the conditions for the ideological hegemony of the bourgeoisie as manifested in the ideologemes of 'there is no alternative' and the 'end of history'.

Furthermore, the bourgeois class struggle was manifested as a global tendency to replace the welfare state model and its Keynesian policies of public investment and state sponsorship of education, healthcare and social security—which was itself a reflection of the capital's need after the Second World War to reinforce investment in infrastructure and reinvigorate the internal market to avoid the intensification of class antitheses and social contradictions—with what is called the 'neoliberal' state. This process took place at a different pace in different countries owing to the unevenness of capitalist development.

The wave of capitalist restructuring measures captured in the neoliberal project started in the two main imperialist centres of the last two centuries—Britain and the United States—where the working-class movement always faced a combination of measures and policies that restricted its autonomous movement, namely, wave after wave of repression and anti-communist legislation combined with the phenomenon of labour aristocracy and the erosion of the militant aspects of the workers' movement. It gradually spread over to the totality of capitalist states, hitting hard the deflated working-class movement. This series of measures was essential to restore the profitability of capital. With the emphasis placed on deregulation of labour relations, proliferation of part-time jobs and workplace flexibility, as well as anti-trade-union legislation, it created even more obstacles to working-class organisation.

It is in this context that the last capitalist crisis erupted and facilitated the implementation of neoliberal measures—including the abolition of collective bargaining, the restriction of the right to strike, the privatisation of social security systems, health care and other social resources—in a number of countries. The measures that dealt with the crisis were met with popular resistance manifested in the Occupy movements in Britain and the U.S.A. and the *indignados* movement in Spain and Greece. It is not surprising that theories identifying popular decision-making as 'the road to tyranny' became popular again. The justification of these measures was carried out predominantly on the basis of an economic and technocratic rationality. According to it, the political decisions concerning the orientation of economic development, the aims of economic production and the regulation of labour relations should be left to experts and not be subject to the choices of an irresponsible and easily manipulated electorate.

Of course, such views and practices had become dominant in the Western world decades before the crisis of 2008. Writing almost forty years ago, Poulantzas noted that, in the contemporary phase of imperialism, the State undergoes considerable modification which—for lack or a better term—he called 'authoritarian statism'.[4] This form is characterised by an intensified control over every sphere of socio-economic life, radical decline of the institutions of political democracy, and draconian and multiform curtailment of the 'formal' liberties.[5] According to Poulantzas, this state form is neither a new form of dictatorial state nor the transitional form on the road to such a State: it rather represents the new democratic form of the bourgeois republic in the current phase of capitalism.

A similar term to describe this state form was coined by Herman Heller in 1932: 'authoritarian liberalism'.[6] According to the doctrine of authoritarian liberalism, representative democracy has to be curtailed to protect economic liberalism and respect for fiscal discipline. This term signifies one of the most current forms of bourgeois class dictatorship. It signifies the transformation of the democratic state form, which accompanies the need to insulate decision-making processes from the popular strata and restrict access of the latter to the former. This form

---

4 Poulantzas, *State, Power, Socialism*, 203.
5 Ibid.
6 Hermann Heller, 'Authoritarian Liberalism?', 21 *European Law Journal*, 295.

of bourgeois class dictatorship is arguably reflected in the structure of the European Union.[7] In fact, it has been argued that the 'often-lamented democratic deficit of European governance' is not a design fault, but rather the result of viewing democracy as an impediment to the achievement of a free labour economy.[8] According to this argument, the E.U. politico-economic paradigm, 'a post-democratic, or better perhaps a-democratic, Hayekian capitalism' is an updated version of ordoliberalism because it insulates the market economy from democratic politics.[9] The new element that the E.U. economic constitution adds to the forms of bourgeois class dictatorship is the multiscalar nature of shifts. To restrict the accessibility of popular strata, the E.U. superstructure allows power to be shifted not only horizontally, but also vertically. The nodal points of policy elaboration and decision therefore do not shift only from the national parliaments to the executive state apparatuses and the administration (horizontally), but also from the national to supranational level (vertically).[10] Therefore, the neutralisation of social and democratic movements today does not primarily take place through repression, 'but by moving the governance of the political economy to a level where democracy cannot follow, and to institutions constitutionally designed to be exempt from political contestation'.[11]

I argue that the term 'bourgeois class dictatorship', rejected by Poulantzas, is as topical and necessary as ever to help account for this state form. This concept captures the common function of normal and exceptional forms in reproducing capitalist social relations. This approach enables the theorisation of phenomena, such as the E.U. superstructure or the U.S. imperial presidency,[12] as contemporary forms of dictatorship of the bourgeoisie. Under this lens, we might recognise that the main characteristics of the dictatorial form (i.e. the strengthening of the repressive apparatus, the devaluation of parliament and the strengthening of the executive) have to some extent become permanent

---

7 Wolfgang Streeck, 'Heller, Schmitt and the Euro', 21 *European Law Journal*, 361; see also M. A. Wilkinson, 'Authoritarian Liberalism in the European: Constitutional Imagination: Second Time as Farce?', 21 *European Law Journal*, 313; Bonefeld, *European Economic Constitution*, 867.
8 Bonefeld, *European Economic Constitution*, 869.
9 Streeck, *Heller, Schmitt and the Euro*, 365.
10 S. Sandbeck and E. Schneider, 'From the Sovereign Debt Crisis to Authoritarian Statism: Contradictions of the European State Project', 2014 *New Political Economy*, 847–871, 865.
11 Streeck, *Heller, Schmitt and the Euro*, 365.
12 See Arthur M. Schlesinger, *The Imperial Presidency* (Boston: Mariner Books, 2004); as well as Steven G. Calabresi and Christopher S. Yoo, *The Unitary Executive* (New Haven: Yale University Press, 2008).

Contribution to the theory of dictatorship 113

characteristics of the liberal democratic form, that is, elements of bourgeois juridico-political normality.

Concerning the strengthening of repressive mechanisms, the changes in criminal legislation over the last twenty years have led to the formation of a legal arsenal necessary for the bourgeoisie to safeguard its rule in the event of a sudden rise in popular discontent due to intensified socio-economic contradictions. The reactionary content of criminal legislation was determined by the goal of targeting terrorism and the subsequent adoption of counter-terrorist legislation. According to the E.U. definition of terrorism, acts of terrorism can be regarded as 'acts which may seriously damage a country or an international organization' with the aim of (*inter alia*) 'seriously destabilising or destroying the fundamental political, constitutional, economic or social structures of a country or an international organisation'.[13] Even a narrow interpretation of this definition, let alone an expansive one, does not preclude social movements and parties that have as their strategic objective radical anti-capitalist social change, as well as national liberation movements, from being regarded as terrorist.

Additionally, through the development of the counter-terrorist legal framework, the concept of suspect has re-emerged in European Union criminal legislation, as well as the possibility of criminalising ideas, since suspects include not only categories of persons related to common crime but also political and activist groups. The four pillars of the 'E.U. Counter-Terrorism Strategy', which was adopted by the European Council in 2005, are 'Prevent, Protect, Pursue, and Respond'.[14] Central among these is the principle of prevention. This principle is intended to prevent people from supporting or turning to terrorism and to stop the next generation of terrorists from emerging. One of the key ways to achieve this goal is by combating ideologies that support 'terrorism', 'extremism' and 'radicalization'.

It is obvious that these concepts are subject to the interpretation of the particular prosecution authorities. In Britain, for instance, the E.U.'s strategy is reflected in the constantly updated CONTEST strategy,[15] which oversees, *inter alia*, the preventive suppression of 'radical' ideas in universities (i.e. in a domain of public discourse where freedom of thought and freedom of speech are essential prerequisites). It is also

---

13 See E.U. Council framework decision on combating terrorism, 2002/475/JHA.
14 Βλέπε, The European Union Counter-Terrorism Strategy, 14469/4/05, REV 4.
15 See 'CONTEST: The United Kingdom's Strategy for Countering Terrorism', June 2018, available at www.gov.uk/government/publications/counter-terrorism-strategy-contest-2018.

important to refer in this context to a recent Report published in July 2019 and funded with a grant from the U.K. Commission for Countering Extremism, which concluded that 'the revolutionary workerist ideology ... may from a certain point of view be considered extremist in and of itself'.[16] It is not a stretch to conclude from this that the criminalisation of revolutionary and radical ideas has already returned to modern legal reality.

Last but not least, reference has to be made to the legal framework that is meant to restrict, control and potentially suppress public protest, as well as advanced forms of social struggle, such as industrial action. Such legislation has been developed in big imperialist centres before spreading to other countries. The exercise of the right to protest in Britain is regulated by the Public Order Act. Part 3 of this Act restricts the exercise of this right by imposing conditions meant to 'prevent serious public disorder, serious criminal damage or serious disruption to the life of the community'. It is obvious that this provision gives wide discretion to the authorities to restrict (section 12) and even prohibit (section 13) the exercise of a right that is of vital importance for popular protest and social struggle. Similarly, the imposition of restrictions on the exercise of the right to strike with the Trade Union Act of 2016 has been exported to other countries and is considered by the E.U. as 'best practice'.[17]

We conclude that even in conditions of normality and unhindered reproduction of the liberal democratic form, the preparation and reinforcement of repressive mechanisms continues undiminished, at both legal and operational levels. Regarding the latter, reference can be made to N.A.T.O.'s crisis management exercises that are regularly and permanently carried out and involve the deployment of armed forces in civil–military scenarios, set in a hybrid environment. These scenarios include hybrid threats, such as climate change disasters, refugee flows and public protests following social unrest. Such exercises are carried out in the context of N.A.T.O.'s new strategic concept and under the auspices of the E.U., which has already recognised the importance of countering such threats.[18]

---

16 See Daniel Allington, Siobhan McAndrew, and David Hirsh, *Violent Extremist Tactics and the Ideology of the Sectarian Far Left*, July 2019, available at: https://assets.publishing.service.gov.uk/government/uploads/system/uploads/attachment_data/file/834429/Allington-McAndrew-Hirsh-2019-Jul-19.pdf.
17 See Dimitrios Kivotidis, 'Theses on the Relationship between Rights and Social Struggle', 70 *Northern Ireland Legal Quarterly*, 407.
18 See E.U. Council Conclusions on Complementary Efforts to Enhance Resilience and Counter Hybrid Threats, 14972/19.

The other characteristic feature of the dictatorial form that has now developed into an element of bourgeois juridico-political normality is the strengthening of executive powers and the devaluation of parliament. This tendency to strengthen executive decision-making, to remove political economic decisions from the popular verdict, and to promote the 'general interest' based on the knowledge of 'experts' has been an inherent feature of the bourgeois state. Institutionally it originated in the interwar period, when a peculiar 'state of emergency' was invoked within the context of the liberal-democratic form. Reference to Roosevelt's first term as President of the United States is pertinent here. In his inaugural address as President, Roosevelt used the language of necessity to justify the increased powers sought from Congress to address the consequences of the capitalist crisis of the 1930s. In particular, he referred to the 'normal balance of executive and legislative authority' which was 'wholly adequate to meet the unprecedented task'. He also referred to the 'unprecedented demand and need for undelayed action' which could lead to a 'temporary departure from that normal balance of public procedure'. On this basis, he asked the Congress 'for the one remaining instrument to meet the crisis—broad Executive power to wage a war against the emergency, as great as the power that would be given to me if we were in fact invaded by a foreign foe'.[19]

This peculiar state of emergency, without amounting to a dictatorial form *tout court*, but entailing, nonetheless, the strengthening of executive power over parliament, was deemed necessary for the capitalist restructuring measures expressed in the New Deal policies. It is worth emphasising that such emergency measures cannot be considered temporary. This is what makes this particular 'state of emergency' peculiar and fully integrated into bourgeois normality. These measures affected the entire economic and social structure of the country. In today's circumstances, by analogy, it would not be strange to invoke a climate emergency to implement the so-called 'Green New Deal' policies. This is a set of proposals that consists of a blend of social-democratic reforms and policies supporting companies that invest in renewable energy and related technologies in their struggle against competing monopolies.[20] The bourgeois intelligentsia is already developing

---

19 See Franklin D. Roosevelt, 'First Inaugural Address', 4 March 1933, available at https://avalon.law.yale.edu/20th_century/froos1.asp.
20 An example of 'Green New Deal' proposals is a Resolution submitted in the U.S. House of Representatives by a number of representatives of the Democratic Party—see H. Res. 109—Recognizing the duty of the Federal Government to create a Green New Deal. This includes proposals such as 'meeting 100 percent of the power demand in the United States through clean, renewable, and zero-emission energy sources' through public investment. To this end it calls on the state to provide for universal

the ideological framework for a possibility of executive implementation of such measures of capitalist restructure.[21]

In all likelihood, the above statement does come as a surprise to the reader. Invoking emergency conditions to adopt measures that are in no way temporary was a daily routine in a series of countries during the financial crisis—a normality that characterized crisis legislation. The devaluation of parliament and the further removal of political decision-making from the people have been key features of the bourgeois response to the recent capitalist crisis.

In a number of countries the invocation of emergency measures was accompanied with the form of the memorandum for the introduction of crisis legislation. The memorandums were the implementation of measures that increased the degree of exploitation of the working class, through the extreme reduction of wages, the deregulation of labour relations and a radical restructuring of the social security system to make it a profitable area for capitalist investment—in short, through the radical reorientation of the economy. In Greece, in particular, all three memorandums (documents of at least 600 pages each, containing a detailed list of measures covering the full range of fiscal and economic policy) were ratified by the Hellenic Parliament through the emergency parliamentary procedure.[22] As a result of the use of this exceptional procedure, there was no substantive public consultation over the reforms. This was justified on the basis that 'it was not possible to accommodate participatory methods when Greece was about to default on its loans'.[23]

The aggressive form of the memorandum accompanied the introduction of equally aggressive measures, which increased the degree of exploitation of the labour force in the name of enhancing 'competitiveness' and attracting investment. The Memorandums of Understanding

---

health-care, higher education and job-creation through public investment. Of course, such political proposals do not constitute 'cracks' in the capitalist economy, as some of their promoters would like to present them. They are rather 'patchwork' that responds to the difficulties the capitalist system faces in managing the contradictions following the crisis.

21 See, for instance, Naomi Klein's book on the subject, *This Changes Everything* (Penguin, 2015). The language of emergency is evident already from the title.
22 Article 109 of the Standing Orders of the Greek Parliament provides that 'if a bill is characterised as urgent, it is processed and examined in one sitting', while 'the debate and passage of the urgent bill is concluded in one meeting which cannot last more than ten hours'. Furthermore, the process of ratification of an Act by the Parliament is characterized as *interna corporis*, and as a result is not subject to judicial review.
23 Aristea Koukiadaki and Lefteris Kretsos, 'Opening Pandora's Box: The Sovereign Debt Crisis and Labour Market Regulation in Greece', 41 *Industrial Law Journal*, 276.

are, therefore, a unity of form and content: a form of implementation of a 'necessary' content, which expresses the fundamental need of the capitalist class to reproduce conditions of profitability in a situation of crisis. The 'exceptional' circumstances of the 'unprecedented crisis' served as justification for the 'rescue' of the Greek, the Spanish, the Irish and the Portuguese economies, but the measures accompanying the 'rescue' were not temporary. Rather, they were justified as necessary to fulfil a normal—and not the least exceptional—obligation of E.U. Member States: fiscal stability and economic policy coordination to achieve 'growth' and 'competitiveness'.[24]

What is more, these class-orientated measures were justified as promoting the public interest. In Greece, the Council of State held that reasons of '*overriding public interest*' necessitated the loan agreement between the Greek government, the IMF and the ECB, and that full compliance with the principles of proportionality and necessity was achieved.[25] The notion of public or general interest (*salus populi*) reveals the link between the normal and the dictatorial form.[26] The principle of *salus populi*, which calls for the formation of a new legal normality for reasons of necessity, refers not only to the salvation of the people but also to its welfare. It may therefore refer not only to matters of life or death but also to the issues of political economy.

The question, however, is: what is the content of the public or general interest? What is in the interest of the people? It is obvious that the answer to this question is determined by the class standpoint of the respondent. From a bourgeois standpoint, the content of public interest is revealed in judgments like the above as consisting of fiscal stability and avoidance of economic disasters. It also includes all of the above

---

24 See E.U. Commission, *Growth, Competitiveness, Employment: The Challenges and Ways Forward into the 21st Century: White Paper*, 1994-03-09.
25 See Judgments 668/2012 and 2307/2014, on the constitutionality of the first and the second Memorandum, respectively.
26 In the U.K. context, these principles have been applied by U.K. courts to justify the reluctance of judges to deal with 'political' questions relating to 'public emergency', 'national security' or 'public interest'. As Lord Carswell put it in the *Bancoult* case, 'a rule of abstinence should apply' and the court should avoid interfering with what is essentially a political judgment. This juridical phenomenon has been central in the development of a 'security state' based on executive decision-making. Indicatively, see *R (Bancoult) v Secretary of State for Foreign and Commonwealth Affairs* [2008] UKHL 61 [109]; *R (Corner House Research) v Director of the Serious Fraud Office* [2008] UKHL 60 [23]; *R (Abbasi) v Secretary of State for Foreign and Commonwealth Affairs* [2002] EWCA Civ 1598; and Thomas Poole's assessment of the above cases under the prism of the category of 'reason of state' (Poole 2015, pp. 262–291).

measures (which result in intensification of exploitation, wealth redistribution from the poorest to the wealthiest, as well as general relative and absolute impoverishment of the majority of the population) that bourgeois theory and institutions consider necessary for the promotion of public interest. Thus, we end up with the paradox that, from a bourgeois standpoint, the welfare of the people is promoted through the exploitation, impoverishment and general deterioration of the standard of living of the people.

On the contrary, if we approach the above questions from a proletarian standpoint, we must begin by recognising that the social contradictions of capitalist society, in particular the fundamental class division between capital and labour, make it impossible for a general interest to exist. The notion of general or public interest performs a very important ideological function by contributing to the reproduction capitalist relations as a legitimating force. This is achieved by obfuscating class divisions and creating a false—but necessary for this reproduction—image of social cohesion.

It is obvious from the above that the institutional framework that conditioned the eruption of the last capitalist crisis, as well as the response to it, cannot be understood unless on the basis of the capitalist tendency towards authoritarian solutions, even if these do not amount to a dictatorial form *tout court*. The general parameter of the capitalist political superstructure is that the economy is not a matter of popular decision-making because it is too important to be left prey to the interests of specific classes and too complex to be dealt with by anyone other than those who have expert knowledge. This parameter enables the characterisation of the spectrum of possible bourgeois juridico-political forms as gradations of authoritarianism. Dictatorship can thus be seen as part of a system of gradations of authoritarianism, the specific form of which is determined by the level of capitalist development and the development of class struggle in specific countries. Insofar as the reproduction of capitalist social relations can be accomplished predominantly on the basis of ideological, consensual means, resort to the dictatorial form is not necessary.

We justifiably arrive at the conclusion that every form of the bourgeois state in the epoch of imperialism consists of authoritarian or potentially dictatorial elements, the degree of manifestation of which ultimately depends on the level of intensification of contradictions and the specific conjuncture of class struggle. The bourgeois state will guarantee the reproduction of capitalist social relations in whatever form, even through violence if need be. Therefore, the dictatorial form, as well as any form of the authoritarian capitalist spectrum, can only be fought not by demanding a return to the normality of a regime based on the rule of law, but by contesting the very property and relations of production that thwart the satisfaction of popular needs and that are reproduced by these gradations of authoritarianism.

6 Theses on the concept of dictatorship

1) The concept of dictatorship denotes either a republican institution whereby liberal freedoms are suspended to deal with a crisis that threatens the reproduction of the state, or a type of regime that involves not just the use of violence and suspension of the law but also a law-generating activity on behalf of the state that may amount to an alteration of the constitutional arrangement. Based on these two types of dictatorial form, different conceptualisations of dictatorship have been advocated (such as Caesaristic dictatorship, Bonapartist dictatorship, classical dictatorship, commissarial dictatorship, sovereign dictatorship, totalitarian dictatorship, etc.).
2) It is hard to separate one type of dictatorship from the other. In fact, one tends to turn into the other. As a distinct form of the bourgeois state, the dictatorial form has historically tended to evolve from a constitutional dictatorship to the establishment of a dictatorial regime *tout court* because of the far-reaching reform necessary to reproduce the bourgeois state in the face of danger. This thesis necessitates an understanding of dictatorship as class rule (i.e. as an essential aspect of the exercise of public power), not in the abstract, but of the political dominance of the ruling class.
3) This means that the concept of dictatorship and the different types of the dictatorial form have to be assessed and can only be understood in their historical context. The dictatorial form and the corresponding conceptualisations exhibit particular characteristics depending on factors, such as: the level of development of capitalist society; the development of repressive and ideological mechanisms of the bourgeois state to ensure the reproduction of capitalist relations; the level of intensification of social and economic contradictions; and the specific conjuncture of class struggle.

4) On this basis, the dictatorial form is understood as an essential form for the reproduction of bourgeois rule and, consequently, of capitalist social relations. The inevitable intensification of socio-economic and political contradictions in the context of capitalist society gives rise to situations of crisis that threaten the reproduction of these relations. Crisis affects the ability of the dominant class to reproduce its rule against its class enemy. It may also give rise to intra-class contradictions and struggle between ruling class factions to achieve a leading role in the dominant bloc. These processes manifest politically in phenomena, such as the proliferation of political parties, distrust for deliberative institutions and devaluation of political parties and parliamentary democracy, as well as proliferation of plebiscitary processes.

5) The dictatorial form refers to a modality of class rule that relies predominantly on violence and repression. This does not mean that ideology and mechanisms for securing consent are not crucial—let alone operative—in this form. On the contrary, the crisis of hegemony and legitimacy tends to lead to a reorganisation of class rule along new principles and institutions. This might entail both a shift of power between the state branches as well as the creation of new foundational principles for legitimating bourgeois rule.

6) *Salus populi suprema lex* is the guiding principle of the dictatorial form. The state's function in a situation of crisis, since ancient Rome, has been ultimately legitimised by the common good or the general or public interest. However, this principle is operative throughout the spectrum of bourgeois juridico-political form. *Salus populi* guides not just the exceptional and dictatorial but also the normal form, as manifested in phenomena of executive decision-making or judicial deference in the context of the liberal-democratic state. A degree of authoritarianism in the name of the common good remains operative even in the most normal, mundane, day-to-day workings of bourgeois state and law. As Schmitt puts it with his concept of the 'ever-present possibility of conflict', the whole spectrum of bourgeois juridico-political forms is authoritarian and potentially dictatorial. We may thus speak of gradations of authoritarianism. This is essentially the meaning of a class dictatorship: a system of repressive and ideological mechanisms that guarantees the reproduction of power, property and production relations as its *ultima ratio*.

7) The concept of class dictatorship is not just about the form of government but about class rule. This is why its analysis cannot be carried out in the abstract, but always in concrete relation to the rule of a specific class: the dictatorship of the bourgeoisie or the dictatorship of the proletariat. The former denotes the historical fact that the fundamental function and purpose of existence of the bourgeois state is to establish, secure, guarantee and reproduce the conditions of capitalist profitability. This function is objective and independent of individual or collective intentions and justifications, insofar as the bourgeois state guarantees the reproduction of capitalist social relations. The analysis of the class context of the dictatorial form confirms the objectivity of the class nature of the bourgeois state, as well as Marx's revolutionary conclusion that the bourgeois state is not an instrument that can be wielded by the workers—it needs to be smashed.

8) Contrary to the dictatorship of the bourgeoisie, which denotes the political rule of the bourgeoisie as well as the role of the bourgeois state in ensuring the reproduction of capitalism, the dictatorship of the proletariat serves a dialectical purpose. It, too, denotes the political rule of the working class and the role of the proletarian state in the process of socialist construction. However, the ultimate purpose of the dictatorship of the proletariat is the development of the conditions for the elimination of classes, as well as the abolition of class rule and the state. The rule of the proletariat, exercised through the proletarian state, is only reproduced so as to lead to the elimination of class rule altogether. The dictatorship of the proletariat refers to the process of long and arduous struggle for the elimination of the socio-economic contradictions inherited from capitalist society. It lasts as long as the state and law wither away (i.e. throughout the historical period of socialist construction, which involves the development of productive forces, social relations, consciousness and habits that will eventually lead to the withering away of state and law).

9) An understanding of the concept of dictatorship of the proletariat resolves, at least theoretically, the antithesis between democracy and dictatorship in bourgeois formalist analyses. Rather than being the antithesis of democracy, the dictatorship of the proletariat strives for the establishment of a fuller democracy (i.e. a substantive democracy whereby the rights of the people are not simply constitutionally enshrined, but the material conditions for their satisfaction are guaranteed). The democratic form of the dictatorship of the proletariat is a unity of form and content. It combines the processes

of political organisation of the working class and the popular strata with the processes of organisation of production and the restructuring of the general material conditions. This thesis shifts the focus from a formalist discussion of democracy and dictatorship to a many-sided understanding of the interwoven processes of political formation and socio-economic change.

Index

authoritarianism: authoritarian liberalism 53, 54, 111; authoritarian statism 2, 111; gradations of authoritarianism 7, 118, 119, 121

class rule 5–7, 9, 14, 36–9, 43–5, 55, 61, 74, 75, 81, 82, 89, 93, 101–8, 120, 121
Committee of Public Safety 18, 30, 31, 33, 73, 74, 102

democracy 1–4, 8, 9, 21, 30, 33, 54, 56, 57, 64, 69, 70, 73–93, 111, 112, 121, 122
despotism 9, 11, 33, 75, 81
dictatorial form 3–7, 28, 40, 52, 58, 63–5, 67, 72, 79, 100, 76, 100–9, 112, 115, 117–22
dictatorial regime 1, 5, 7, 14, 22, 31, 46, 48, 75, 76, 83
dictatorship: Bonapartist dictatorship 36–9, 42–6, 60, 105, 107, 120; Caesaristic dictatorship 10–14, 18, 19, 22, 35, 120; commissarial dictatorship 15, 19–22, 31, 32, 39, 49, 50, 72, 102, 120; constitutional dictatorship 32, 35, 46, 72, 120; fascist dictatorship 36, 38, 58, 60–2, 110; Nazi dictatorship 5, 48, 52, 60, 64–7; sovereign dictatorship 10, 14–22, 30, 31, 40, 49, 50, 64, 103, 104, 120
dictatorship of the bourgeoisie 2, 75, 89, 99, 108, 109, 112, 122

dictatorship of the proletariat 19, 21, 73–9, 83, 84, 89–99, 108, 109, 122
Donoso Cortés, Juan 2, 3, 6, 9, 33

fascism 6, 48, 54, 58–63, 67–71

general interest 7, 22, 27, 28, 115, 117, 118
Gramsci, Antonio 3, 6, 36–9, 59–63, 80

hegemony 6, 38–46, 59–67, 70, 104–6, 110, 121
Hitler 1, 8, 49, 68–70

ideology 33, 38, 43, 51, 56, 58, 63, 64, 80, 90, 105–8, 114, 121

Lenin 47, 73, 74, 78–83, 90–5

martial law 33, 75, 101, 103
Marx, Karl 29, 35, 36, 39–46, 73–81, 91–6

Paris Commune 7, 74–8, 91
Poulantzas, Nicos 2, 6, 39, 46, 58–64, 71, 80–3, 88, 91, 107, 111, 112

repression 38, 39, 43, 48, 60, 63–5, 79, 93, 101, 102, 105, 106, 108–10, 112, 121

salus populi 7, 12, 22, 26–8, 30, 34, 41, 77, 103, 117, 121

sovereignty 2, 16, 17, 20–3, 30, 34, 50, 52, 56, 103
Schmitt, Carl 10, 14–23, 30–4, 42, 48–54, 56, 64, 65, 72, 102–4, 109, 121
Stalin 1, 55, 83, 92, 97, 98
state of emergency 5, 9, 14, 22–5, 48, 101, 115

state of exception 3, 5, 22–6, 48, 49, 58, 64, 65, 71, 101

totalitarianism 1, 3, 48, 53–8, 80
tyranny 9, 33, 111

withering away of the state 74, 93, 122

Taylor & Francis eBooks

www.taylorfrancis.com

A single destination for eBooks from Taylor & Francis with increased functionality and an improved user experience to meet the needs of our customers.

90,000+ eBooks of award-winning academic content in Humanities, Social Science, Science, Technology, Engineering, and Medical written by a global network of editors and authors.

TAYLOR & FRANCIS EBOOKS OFFERS:

- A streamlined experience for our library customers
- A single point of discovery for all of our eBook content
- Improved search and discovery of content at both book and chapter level

REQUEST A FREE TRIAL
support@taylorfrancis.com

For Product Safety Concerns and Information please contact our EU representative GPSR@taylorandfrancis.com
Taylor & Francis Verlag GmbH, Kaufingerstraße 24, 80331 München, Germany

www.ingramcontent.com/pod-product-compliance
Lightning Source LLC
Chambersburg PA
CBHW051752230426
43670CB00012B/2261